D1616777

WITHDRAWN
UTSA LIBRARIES

ALSO BY AMY CLAMPITT

POETRY

The Collected Poems of Amy Clampitt (1997)
A Silence Opens (1994)
Westward (1990)
Archaic Figure (1987)
What the Light Was Like (1985)
The Kingfisher (1983)

CHAPBOOKS

The Isthmus (1981)
Multitudes, Multitudes (1973)

PROSE

Love, Amy: The Selected Letters of Amy Clampitt
edited by Willard Spiegelman (2005)
Predecessors, Et Cetera: Essays (1991)
The Essential Donne (editor) (1988)

Selected Poems

Amy Clampitt

Selected Poems

Edited by Mary Jo Salter

ALFRED A. KNOPF   *New York*   2010

THIS IS A BORZOI BOOK
PUBLISHED BY ALFRED A. KNOPF

Copyright © 2010 by The Estate of Amy Clampitt
Introduction and chronology copyright © 2010 by Mary Jo Salter

All rights reserved. Published in the United States by Alfred A. Knopf,
a division of Random House, Inc., New York, and in Canada
by Random House of Canada Limited, Toronto.

www.aaknopf.com

Knopf, Borzoi Books, and the colophon are registered
trademarks of Random House, Inc.

Some of the poems in this collection originally appeared in the following works:

The Kingfisher, copyright © 1983 by Amy Clampitt (Alfred A. Knopf)
What the Light Was Like, copyright © 1985 by Amy Clampitt (Alfred A. Knopf)
Archaic Figure, copyright © 1987 by Amy Clampitt (Alfred A. Knopf)
Westward, copyright © 1990 by Amy Clampitt (Alfred A. Knopf)
A Silence Opens, copyright © 1993 by Amy Clampitt (Alfred A. Knopf)

"The Equinoctial Disturbances," "Pot Nomads," and
"The Winter Bird" originally appeared in *The New Yorker.*

Library of Congress Cataloguing-in-Publication Data
Clampitt, Amy.
[Poems. Selections]
Selected poems / by Amy Clampitt ; edited by Mary Jo Salter. — 1st ed.
p. cm.
Includes bibliographical references and index.
ISBN 978-0-375-71193-0
I. Salter, Mary Jo.   II. Title.
PS3553.L23A6 2010
811'.54—dc22   2010010707

Manufactured in the United States of America
First Edition

Library
University of Texas
at San Antonio

Contents

Introduction

"Nothing's certain." The first sentence of Amy Clampitt's favorite of her own poems, "A Hermit Thrush," asserts itself with uncharacteristic brevity, and thus with a suggestion of certainty. The paradox is itself characteristic. Throughout her life, Clampitt wavered—not so much between certainty and doubt as among competing, even mutually exclusive certainties.

Insecure, sometimes timorous, she evinced nonetheless an astonishing confidence. Among the things she felt she knew as a wholly unknown writer of thirty-five was that *"I am in it"*—English literature, that is. Such was her claim to a brother ten years younger, a scientist not apt to disagree. She was sixty-three (and a much-rejected fiction writer) when she made good on her claim to fame, with the publication in 1983 of her brilliant first collection of poems, *The Kingfisher*. The book gave her instant promotion to the highest echelons of the poetry establishment. A proud initiate to that club, she did not become any less a skittish, fragile solitary. She was odd, singular; her many friends knew it.

Rebellious, nonconformist, wary of systems of all kinds, she could also be dogmatic. There were different dogmas along the way, and her convictions took evolutionary leaps. Personal freedom, though, was a constant ideal—a goal both supported and thwarted by a Quaker upbringing that was altruistic, cultured, politically liberal, and (her word) "repressed." A footloose single woman in her late twenties, traveling abroad for the first time, she conveyed in her novelistic journal a romantic restlessness as she scanned the young men on shipboard "idly as for a chocolate with just the right flavor." Past thirty, on another trip to England, she was apostate (and adolescent) enough to deplore some "old ladies" who were "very pious, very distasteful to look at." Yet midway through her novel-writing thirties, she experienced the solemn joy of a conversion, turned that mystical moment into a massive poem, considered becoming an Episcopal nun, and for a time wrote daily devotional meditations. In her forties, she left the church with an abruptness that surprised her friends, stopped writing fiction, and turned to nearly round-the-clock liberal activism, in a sort of conversion to political protest. The street demonstrator who had once so thrillingly spent a night in jail then fell in love with a distinguished law professor—although, to complicate the irony, Harold Korn was pretty radical too. In her fifties, she moved in with him, the man of her life; yet she protected her autonomy so fiercely that for years she kept an apartment of her own, rarely used. With Hal's encouragement, by her sixties the private poet had thrown herself wholly into a public, even international, persona. Finally, in her seventies, after decades of claiming she would never marry, she became Hal's bride in her final spring.

A life of warring certainties had its parallel in her contradictory literary approaches. Raised in a time and place of no excess—during the Depression, on the Iowa prairie—she would in her writing implicitly uphold the Quaker values of privacy, dignity, reticence. Her wariness of overexplanation occasionally resulted in obliquity. And yet she was constantly bursting with marveling observations and dizzy pleasures, and equally keen exasperations and desperations, that demanded expression in one genre or another, and whether or not anyone else was reading her words. She wrote long, vivacious, highly publishable letters. (Although some fraction of her correspondence saw print years after her death, her private journals and travel essays, as well as the drafts toward unpublished novels, could fill another bookshelf.)

Having dropped out of graduate studies in English because, she decided, she was no scholar, she later published a book of literary essays and wrote a play grounded in a great deal of (perhaps too evident) literary-historical research. She lived in New York for half a century, but wrote about birds perched on branches at least as much as about passengers on the subway: she was an urban nature poet. She often said she wanted to be modern, and was; but she challenged her contemporaries, both formal and free-verse poets, by divorcing that old married couple rhyme and meter: she eschewed strict meter while often indulging richly in rhyme. She was not only a prolific writer but also a "wordy" one, whose love of language, of folded etymologies and interlocking phonemes, led her to use three words when one might suffice, and to make a virtue of excess. Daring in her poems to say so much, so gorgeously, and in long, syntactically knotted sentences, set her apart in the bare-bones 1980s. Yet for her final volume of poems, published in 1994 just months before her death, she alternated between her usual densely packed style and another, airier, more fragmentary mode, and reaffirmed her Quaker side with the title *A Silence Opens*.

Nothing's certain. "Nothing Stays Put" was another of her titles. She herself didn't stay put—she traveled ceaselessly (and slowly, because of a fear of flying). She did much of her best writing during summer escapes from New York to the coast of Maine, where she was glad to depict not only the roiling seascape before her but also the flat, often desolate landscapes of her Iowa childhood. She wrote with a formidable knowledge of American history, particularly of our expansion westward, but could be, she admitted, a snob in her preference for things European. Modern Greece, classical Greek, Greek myth, all spoke to her vividly. British literary biography did, too. She brought to fruition some of her most complex thoughts by grafting them onto the lives and writings of George Eliot, Virginia Woolf, John Keats, William and Dorothy Wordsworth, Samuel Taylor Coleridge. (Her stylistic models also included John Donne, Gerard Manley Hopkins, Emily Dickinson, Marianne Moore.)

In her imagination she disregarded the unities of time, place, and action, and—to append a fourth unity to Aristotle's trio—character. Two of her longest, most admired poems, "Beethoven, Opus 111," and "The Prairie," show her daring to fuse humble, familiar characters with the distant and elevated—her farmer father with Beethoven, and her Pasadena-born grandfather with Chekhov. Meanwhile, year after year, the tide and the fog entered and exited the stage of her Maine poems. The unforeseeable, unrepeatable performances ranged from her little confection "Sea Mouse" to the grave title poem of her second book, a fisherman's elegy she called "What the Light Was Like."

In poems the size of postcards ("Birdham") and letters ("Losing Track of Language"), Clampitt could produce travel writing amusingly and incisively. Pilgrimages—by drivers on the interstate ("A Procession at Candlemas"), or by saint's-day pedestrians in Italy ("Matrix")—provoked some of her deeper yearnings and sorrows. Seedings, transplantings, dispersals—of houseplants that did, or didn't, survive and of weeds that wouldn't stop flourishing—prompted her again and again to write. Most ambitiously, she wrote of exile, particularly of the often tragic movements of peoples in the nineteenth and twentieth centuries. Called upon to describe herself in an interview, she said she was "a poet of displacement."

Amy Clampitt seldom relied on argumentation. In her life (and I knew her well) she had strong opinions, and these made their way into her poetry, but opinions are not arguments. Displacement was not merely her major theme but also a major poetic device. You couldn't be sure where her thought was going; instead, you were invited to participate in her well-phrased wonder at where you both arrived. Hers was not a logical but an associative mind. While introducing information or imagery, her poems often looped back with an exploratory aplomb to repeat clauses and lines, thus attaching new meanings to old gestures. Those meanings were rarely susceptible to paraphrase, and she negotiated paradox beautifully. Her genius was to stir unlikely figures, themes, and sounds into each other boldly, even rashly, and to contain, in well-crafted vessels, their chemical reactions.

In *A Silence Opens,* "Sed de Correr" is a notable example of that technique; or, to change the metaphor from chemistry to architecture, the poem is one of her most venturesome, and successful, edifices. Built of bending fragments of syntax, of pointedly strange likenesses that, in repetition and transformation, become somehow natural, it's a Bilbao Guggenheim of a poem. The Spanish title, a phrase by César Vallejo literally meaning "a thirst for running," is translated by Clampitt as "the urge to disjoin, the hunger/to have gone, to be going." Often having given voice to the giddiness and pain of leaving previous selves behind, she found no subject closer to her heart than, as she phrases it here, "running away from what made one." She links unpretentiously her young self, a sort of immigrant from Iowa to Greenwich Village, with Federico García Lorca arriving as a foreigner in Harlem.

First, though, "Sed de Correr" recollects the "ash tree outside the schoolroom" of her childhood. In the phallic metaphor of "the great, growing / trunk of it hardening, the mass, the circumference," Clampitt establishes a theme, the puzzling, fearful power of sexual desire. But like the tree, the poem keeps branching. The natural image seen from the schoolroom window yields to a man-made one, of looming New York buildings with rows of windows—"the lit grid's apertures past counting." She imagines Lorca looking out at the "bleared eyeholes" of the jailed, and at windows behind which, not looking out but in, "the mad / are warehoused." (Clampitt's sister, surely thought of here but unmentioned, was a sometimes-institutionalized schizophrenic.) In Clampitt's own city apartment, "the starry apertures of paperwhite narcissus" are her only "opening," "a sweetness I drank at as though entity / might depend from it." Note her habitual accuracy: entity depends *from*, not *on;* paperwhites "depend" in hanging down from their own slight weight.

The repeated word "aperture" soon takes us to Virginia Woolf: "the lighthouse, / its pulsing aperture engulfed, / the waves breaking." That's a highly sexualized version, you'd have to say, of the lighthouse Woolf presented as a symbol for (in part) art itself. Clampitt's next stanza delivers the waters joining over Woolf's head: her suicide by drowning, large stone in her pocket. A moment later we face Kafka's "windowless / warren of calculation, contingency, foresight." The cockroaches of the city ("those feelers, that lustrous, chitinous / lodging among interstices, among systems / we've lost track of the workings of") have become, by implication, all the denizens of Kafka's nightmare bureaucracies as well as poor, peculiar Gregor Samsa of "The Metamorphosis." Clampitt's own metamorphoses of imagery lead us by stanza's end to consider, in a gathering list, "the gathering impasse of language, the screech / of its decibels, the mumble of its circumlocutions, / the mutter, all over Europe" of a world war that America is about to enter.

But the poem is only half over, its meanings only partly opened. By the end, it is about—what is "about" about, anyway?—failed political systems that create exiles and runaways, and lost innocence: our lost accounts, that is, of most of innocence and experience. We are on the move, all of us; we cannot memorialize the whole of life in words; the words we do write miss the mark; and they cannot all be preserved. The adolescent's gaze on the sexually charged Iowa "ash tree outside the schoolroom" has transmuted into the young adult's discovery, from "a window / onto an airshaft," of two men making love ("I'd not / known how it was done"), and, finally, into a mature woman's consideration of a dying tree on West Twelfth Street, whose "leaves" are the writer's pages. In the poem's concluding lines, the delicate "paperwhite narcissus" we had learned of many lines before has blossomed fully into the narcissism of the writer's quest to be remembered on paper:

> The axe is laid
> at the root of the ash tree. The leaves of dispersal,
> the runaway pages, surround us. Who
> will hear? Who will gather
> them in? Who will read them?

This selection of poems is a gathering; but it is a winnowing, too. The challenge, here, was to reduce Amy Clampitt's poems by about half. All anthologizing has its quandaries, but with Clampitt the problem is not in her having written many more poems of importance than she published in book form. She did write a great deal, including poems for two early chapbooks (*Multitudes, Multitudes* of 1973 and *The Isthmus* of 1981), but these slim, engaging volumes contain no poem, in my view, that is "better" than those I have regretfully excised here from the five full-length books Knopf published in her lifetime.

I have tried to follow the spirit of Amy Clampitt's practice. She could have resurrected poems from her chapbooks, but did not. In the correspondence of our friendship, which coincided closely with her published writing career, I watched her delete from and rearrange every book manuscript with her habitually severe eye. She was wary of minor productions, and had to be persuaded to publish in book form some of her shorter delights, such as the rhyme tour de force "Exmoor" or the sly sonnet "The Cormorant in Its Element."

Perhaps her anthologist's hardest choice is what to do about long, multipart poems, as well as separate poems clearly meant to be read as a thematic unit. To keep all such sequences intact for this selected edition, while omitting many smaller, stand-alone poems, would perhaps give the false impression that she produced mostly blockbusters. On the other hand, because her longer poems usually make use of nonfiction—of historical and biographical contexts—any one part isolated for publication runs the risk of looking deracinated.

I have compromised by including the whole of one masterly eight-poem sequence, "Voyages: A Homage to John Keats," for its intrinsic beauty and for other reasons: Clampitt's lifelong obsession with Keats's truncated career, her style's great affinities with that young (mature) poet's, and her engagement with Romantic poetry as a whole. Some, but not all, of her poems about Wordsworth and his circle (Dorothy Wordsworth, ultimately, interested her most) and about George Eliot are reproduced here. Clampitt's long sequence "The Mirror of the Gorgon" responded to a trip to Greece and, more deeply, to a fascination with Medusa that she felt from an early age. Yet even to accommodate all the "Gorgon" poems would be too limiting: they extend beyond the named sequence.

A recording survives of one of Clampitt's public readings, probably in 1986–87, in which she had been asked to integrate, with commentary, some of her own work with choices from Emily Dickinson's poems. "The Soul selects her own Society—" begins one of these. When the soul, at the end of Dickinson's poem, closes "the Valves of her attention / Like Stone—," Clampitt says she thinks of "people turning to stone" and the Medusa myth. From there Clampitt invites her audience to consider an incident in the life of George Eliot, who feared she could herself be called a Medusa. We are then led to Clampitt's poem "Hippocrene," named for "the pool that was stamped by the winged horse, Pegasus, who was born of the decapitated corpse of Medusa." In Clampitt's poem, the Hippocrene lives on in Virginia Woolf's England, as a symbol of the uncrossable waters of despair. Clampitt reads the poem to her audience, and notes its citation from Woolf's novel *The Waves:* "I came to the puddle. I could not cross it. Identity failed me. We are nothing, I said, and fell."

That, in a nutshell, is how Amy Clampitt thought. Separating one poem from its fellows in such an oeuvre is an exercise doomed to frustration—much like plucking just one or two independent lines from a ten-line Clampitt sentence.

I have plucked just four of Clampitt's uncollected poems to be printed here. An excerpt from the long, never-published "The Sun on the Stone" is the first. It celebrates her spiritual awakening in 1956, but hardly limits itself to Christian imagery. Following Milton, one of her heroes, Clampitt makes seamless transitions between classical and Christian tropes; the stone here that belongs to the Cloisters, in New York, belongs also to the Medusa myth.

Of a number of poems remaining in her papers, three were published in *The New Yorker* after Clampitt's final book had gone to press. "The Equinoctial Disturbances" was followed, after her death, by "Pot Nomads" and "The Winter Bird." "The Equinoctial Disturbances" is a haunting example of Clampitt's late style—or one of her styles, in which spaces appear mid-line and punctuation is minimized. She presents the confusions inherent in illness and insomnia, but does so in a way that is artistically anything but confused:

> Pain Management arrives
> dressed all in green
> a rosebud in (can morphine
> have invented this)
> its buttonhole
>
> Oncology

Much more could be said about each of the three poems, but I will confine myself to "Pot Nomads." It is less shapely than her finest work; written in a terminal patient's haste, it conveys her fear that, like her houseplants, she won't "make it through the winter." Yet this poem offers a captivating look at her enduring preoccupations.

Clampitt's poetry is as thickly carpeted with flowers as a tapestry. Among her favorite blooms, violets emerge as a personal emblem for beginnings and endings, births and deaths. As she noted in an essay called "Providence," her earliest memory dated from the April day a brother was born. A bed of blue violets beckoned from "the outermost grove," violets whose intensity of hue she compared to a body of water. (True blue itself seemed to have had for her a psychic pull. I think of her account of meeting her future husband, Hal, whose face was so seriously scarred by burns that some people turned away from it. From across the room she had been attracted, she told me, by his "beautiful blue eyes." She praises those eyes, too, in her poem "Blueberrying in August.")

Violets pop up conspicuously in her poems about George Eliot. That pseudonymous novelist who cohabitated scandalously with (as Clampitt made sure to specify) a "pockmarked" drama critic was in some ways an alter ego for the good-as-anonymous poet who met the disfigured, enlightened man Hal Korn and moved in with him. In "George Eliot Country," the "violets still bloom" beside the church where Mary Ann Evans was christened; in another Clampitt poem, "Highgate Cemetery," Edith Simcox, Eliot's idolatrous mourner, arrives at the funeral "with a nosegay of violets" and becomes distracted by grief. She "came to herself finally / at a station she didn't recognize, / somewhere in Hampstead." *Came to herself:* that might be a motto for both Eliot and Clampitt.

In "Pot Nomads"—set in April, the budding month of her first memory—the "yardful" of violets are purple. Clampitt has also been tending some potted primulas—as their etymology tells us, the first flowers of spring. She is, she admits, irresponsible with them: "Left unwatered while I / gallivanted elsewhere, / they'd languish." (It is typically high-spirited of her to present travel as entertainment. She had been shuttling to chemotherapy appointments by the time of this poem's composition.) The poet is herself, evidently, like the indoor primulas that "would droop and then, repeatedly, / revive, put out new blooms, / bright nurslings of nothing but / the sun and more tap water." At last the "tough" and "warty" primulas are returned to the ground, and months later, in a fall weeding, she rediscovers them "greenly / holding on": ironically, in being buried and forgotten (their "travels over"), they have a greater chance at survival than in her keeping.

The experienced Clampitt reader will see "Pot Nomads" hearkening to earlier poems that find in the taming of plants a way to get at something grander. The tragic "Sed de Correr," with its paperwhites, is on that reading list. So is "High Culture," whose amaryllis blooms are compared to a "somewhat / famous violinist" paying a visit to the "parlor of the farmhouse." So is "The Horned Rampion," in which a long-forgotten, dried wildflower rediscovered between pages of the *Encyclopedia Britannica* is like "old love / reopened, still quivering."

Another in this nursery of poems is "A Hedge of Rubber Trees"—chatty, long-lined, busy with apparently trivial detail, and terribly sad. The rubber trees of the poem's title are potted. They serve as window shades in the Brooklyn apartment of an eccentric friend, a woman of "threadbare history" who has washed up from somewhere in the "Baltic cold" (and who drinks—she might be called potted, too). She lives, and by poem's end has apparently died, surrounded by the rubber trees, three cats, a canary, and cockroaches. Clampitt writes of her initial empathy with the friend whom she later, guiltily, loses track of:

> Unclassifiable castoffs, misfits, marginal cases:
> when you're one yourself, or close to it, there's
> a reassurance you haven't quite gone
> under by taking up with somebody odder than you are.

In a *Paris Review* interview of 1993, Clampitt, now a famous poet, connected this poem to the biographical sketches of her apprentice chapbook *Multitudes, Multitudes*: poems about survivors, particularly female ones. "The lives of marginal, overlooked, and neglected women have a kind of analogue in growing things," she said, "the weeds that spring up in vacant lots and are the precise opposite of the showy, carefully cultivated blooms in a florist's window." She maintained in the interview that she was "put off" by militant women. And she was not a "feminist poet." But was she, if pressed, a feminist? Yes.

"Pot Nomads" also evokes Clampitt's "Beethoven, Opus 111." In the final, extended stanza of that great poem, she shifts from describing Beethoven's piano music to recounting a seemingly minor roadside incident in her father's life. And she does so abruptly in mid-line, with her own technique's "astonishment of sweetness":

> a disintegrating surf of blossom
> opening along the keyboard, along the fencerows
> the astonishment of sweetness. My father,
> driving somewhere in Kansas or Colorado,
> in dustbowl country, stopped the car
> to dig up by the roots a flower
> he'd never seen before—

A few lines later, Clampitt adds,

> He mentioned in a letter the disappointment
> of his having hoped it might transplant—
> an episode that brings me near tears,
> still, as even his dying does not.

And he asks from his hospital bed that someone "take away the flowers." To his daughter, that wish was tantamount to death itself.

In this book I have repotted some of Amy Clampitt's most vital poems, in the hope of seeing them flourish in new surroundings. "Nothing's certain," in an existence she called "this / botched, cumbersome, much-mended, / not unsatisfactory thing." That a great many of Amy Clampitt's poems will continue to thrive, one way or another, is about as certain as things get.

—Mary Jo Salter

from THE KINGFISHER

(1983)

THE COVE

Inside the snug house, blue willow-ware
plates go round the dado, cross-stitch
domesticates the guest room, whole nutmegs
inhabit the spice rack, and when there's fog
or a gale we get a fire going, listen
to Mozart, read Marianne Moore, or
sit looking out at the eiders, trig
in their white-over-black as they tip
and tuck themselves into the swell, almost
as though diving under the eiderdown
in a *gemütlich* hotel room at Innsbruck.

At dusk we watch a porcupine, hoary
quadruped, emerge from under the spruce trees,
needle-tined paddle tail held out straight
behind, as though the ground were negotiable
only by climbing, to examine the premises,
and then withdraw from the (we presume)
alarming realm of the horizontal into
the up-and-down underbrush of normality.

From the sundeck, overhung by a gale-
hugged mountain ash, limbs blotched
and tufted with lichen, where in good
weather, every time we look up there's
a new kind of warbler flirting, all ombré
and fine stitchery, through the foliage,
one midday, looking down at the grass
we noticed a turtle—domed repoussé
leather with an underlip of crimson—
as it hove eastward, a covered
wagon intent on the wrong direction.

Where at low tide the rocks, like the
back of an old sheepdog or spaniel, are
rugg'd with wet seaweed, the cove
embays a pavement of ocean, at times

wrinkling like tinfoil, at others
all isinglass flakes, or sun-pounded
gritty glitter of mica; or hanging
intact, a curtain wall just frescoed
indigo, so immense a hue, a blue
of such majesty it can't be looked at,
at whose apex there pulses, even
in daylight, a lighthouse, light-
pierced like a needle's eye.

FOG

A vagueness comes over everything,
as though proving color and contour
alike dispensable: the lighthouse
extinct, the islands' spruce-tips
drunk up like milk in the
universal emulsion; houses
reverting into the lost
and forgotten; granite
subsumed, a rumor
in a mumble of ocean.
                              Tactile
definition, however, has not been
totally banished: hanging
tassel by tassel, panicled
foxtail and needlegrass,
dropseed, furred hawkweed,
and last season's rose-hips
are vested in silenced
chimes of the finest,
clearest sea-crystal.
                              Opacity
opens up rooms, a showcase
for the hueless moonflower
corolla, as Georgia
O'Keeffe might have seen it,
of foghorns; the nodding
campanula of bell buoys;
the ticking, linear
filigree of bird voices.

GRADUAL CLEARING

Late in the day the fog
wrung itself out like a sponge
in glades of rain,
sieving the half-invisible
cove with speartips;
then, in a lifting
of wisps and scarves, of smoke-rings
from about the islands, disclosing
what had been wavering
fishnet plissé as a smoothness
of peau-de-soie or just-ironed
percale, with a tatting
of foam out where the rocks are,
the sheened no-color of it,
the bandings of platinum
and magnesium suffusing,
minute by minute, with clandestine
rose and violet, with opaline
nuance of milkweed, a texture
not to be spoken of above a whisper,
began, all along the horizon,
gradually to unseal
like the lip of a cave
or of a cavernous,
single, pearl-
engendering seashell.

THE OUTER BAR

When through some lacuna, chink, or interstice
in the unlicensed free-for-all that goes
on without a halt out there all day, all night,
all through the winter,

one morning at low tide you walk dry-shod across
a shadow isthmus to the outer bar,
you find yourself, once over, sinking at every step
into a luscious mess—

a vegetation of unbarbered, virgin, foot-thick
velvet, the air you breathe an aromatic
thicket, odors in confusion starting up
at every step like partridges

or schools of fishes, an element you swim through
as to an unplanned, headily illicit
interview. The light out there, gashed
by the surf's scimitar,

is blinding, a rebuke—Go back! Go back!—
behind the silhouetted shipwreck (Whose?
When did it happen? Back in the village
nobody can tell you),

the bell buoy hunkering knee-deep in foam,
a blood-red-painted harbinger. How strange
a rim, back where you came from,
of familiar portents

reviewed from this *isola bella*, paradise
inside a prison rockpile—the unravished
protégé of guardians so lawless, refuge
moated up in such a shambles!

Your mind keeps turning back to look at them—
chain-gang archangels that in their prismatic
frenzy fall, gall and gash the daylight
out there, all through the winter.

SEA MOUSE

The orphanage of possibility
has had to be expanded to
admit the sea mouse. No one
had asked for such a thing,
or prophesied its advent,

sheltering under ruching
edges of sea lettuce—
a wet thing but pettable
as, seen in the distance,
the tops of copses,

sun-honeyed, needle-pelted
pine trees, bearded barley,
or anything newborn not bald
but furred. No rodent this
scabrous, this unlooked-for

foundling, no catnip plaything
for a cat to worry, not even
an echinoderm, the creature
seems to be a worm. Silk-spiny,
baby-mummy-swaddled, it's

at home where every corridor
is mop-and-bucket scrubbed
and aired from wall to wall
twice daily by the inde-
fatigable tidal head nurse.

BEACH GLASS

While you walk the water's edge,
turning over concepts
I can't envision, the honking buoy
serves notice that at any time
the wind may change,
the reef-bell clatters
its treble monotone, deaf as Cassandra
to any note but warning. The ocean,
cumbered by no business more urgent
than keeping open old accounts
that never balanced,
goes on shuffling its millenniums
of quartz, granite, and basalt.
                It behaves
toward the permutations of novelty—
driftwood and shipwreck, last night's
beer cans, spilt oil, the coughed-up
residue of plastic—with random
impartiality, playing catch or tag
or touch-last like a terrier,
turning the same thing over and over,
over and over. For the ocean, nothing
is beneath consideration.
              The houses
of so many mussels and periwinkles
have been abandoned here, it's hopeless
to know which to salvage. Instead
I keep a lookout for beach glass—
amber of Budweiser, chrysoprase
of Almadén and Gallo, lapis
by way of (no getting around it,
I'm afraid) Phillips'
Milk of Magnesia, with now and then a rare
translucent turquoise or blurred amethyst
of no known origin.
             The process
goes on forever: they came from sand,

they go back to gravel,
along with the treasuries
of Murano, the buttressed
astonishments of Chartres,
which even now are readying
for being turned over and over as gravely
and gradually as an intellect
engaged in the hazardous
redefinition of structures
no one has yet looked at.

MARINE SURFACE, LOW OVERCAST

Out of churned aureoles
this buttermilk, this
herringbone of albatross,
floss of mercury,
déshabille of spun
aluminum, furred with a velouté
of looking-glass,

a stuff so single
it might almost be lifted,
folded over, crawled underneath
or slid between, as nakedness-
caressing sheets, or donned
and worn, the train-borne
trapping of an unrepeatable
occasion,

this wind-silver
rumpling as of oatfields,
a suede of meadow,
a nub, a nap, a mane of lustre
lithe as the slide
of muscle in its
sheath of skin,

laminae of living tissue,
mysteries of flex,
affinities of texture,
subtleties of touch, of pressure
and release, the suppleness
of long and intimate
association,

new synchronies of fingertip,
of breath, of sequence,
entities that still can rouse,
can stir or solder,

whip to a froth, or force
to march in strictly
hierarchical formation

down galleries of sheen, of flux,
cathedral domes that seem to hover
overturned and shaken like a basin
to the noise of voices,
from a rustle to the jostle
of such rush-hour
conglomerations

no loom, no spinneret, no forge, no factor,
no process whatsoever, patent
applied or not applied for,
no five-year formula, no fabric
for which pure imagining,
except thus prompted,
can invent the equal.

THE SUN UNDERFOOT
AMONG THE SUNDEWS

An ingenuity too astonishing
to be quite fortuitous is
this bog full of sundews, sphagnum-
lined and shaped like a teacup.
                                    A step
down and you're into it; a
wilderness swallows you up:
ankle-, then knee-, then midriff-
to-shoulder-deep in wetfooted
understory, an overhead
spruce-tamarack horizon hinting
you'll never get out of here.
                                    But the sun
among the sundews, down there,
is so bright, an underfoot
webwork of carnivorous rubies,
a star-swarm thick as the gnats
they're set to catch, delectable
double-faced cockleburs, each
hair-tip a sticky mirror
afire with sunlight, a million
of them and again a million,
each mirror a trap set to
unhand unbelieving,
                          that either
a First Cause said once, "Let there
be sundews," and there were, or they've
made their way here unaided
other than by that backhand, round-
about refusal to assume responsibility
known as Natural Selection.
                                    But the sun
underfoot is so dazzling
down there among the sundews,
there is so much light
in the cup that, looking,
you start to fall upward.

ON THE DISADVANTAGES
OF CENTRAL HEATING

cold nights on the farm, a sock-shod
stove-warmed flatiron slid under
the covers, mornings a damascene-
sealed bizarrerie of fernwork
          decades ago now

waking in northwest London, tea
brought up steaming, a Peek Frean
biscuit alongside to be nibbled
as blue gas leaps up singing
          decades ago now

damp sheets in Dorset, fog-hung
habitat of bronchitis, of long
hot soaks in the bathtub, of nothing
quite drying out till next summer:
          delicious to think of

hassocks pulled in close, toasting-
forks held to coal-glow, strong-minded
small boys and big eager sheepdogs
muscling in on bookish profundities
          now quite forgotten

the farmhouse long sold, old friends
dead or lost track of, what's salvaged
is this vivid diminuendo, unfogged
by mere affect, the perishing residue
          of pure sensation

A PROCESSION AT CANDLEMAS

Moving on or going back to where you came from,
bad news is what you mainly travel with:
a breakup or a breakdown, someone running off

or walking out, called up or called home:
death in the family. Nudged from their stanchions
outside the terminal, anonymous of purpose

as a flock of birds, the bison of the highway
funnel westward onto Route 80, mirroring
an entity that cannot look into itself and know

what makes it what it is. Sooner or later
every trek becomes a funeral procession.
The mother curtained in Intensive Care—

a scene the mind leaves blank, fleeing instead
toward scenes of transhumance, the belled sheep
moving up the Pyrenees, red-tasseled pack llamas

footing velvet-green precipices, the Kurdish
women, jingling with bangles, gorgeous
on their rug-piled mounts—already lying dead,

bereavement altering the moving lights
to a processional, a feast of Candlemas.
Change as child-bearing, birth as a kind

of shucking off: out of what began
as a Mosaic insult—such a loathing
of the common origin, even a virgin,

having given birth, needs purifying—
to carry fire as though it were a flower,
the terror and the loveliness entrusted

into naked hands, supposing God might have,
might actually need a mother: people have
at times found this a way of being happy.

A Candlemas of moving lights along Route 80;
lighted candles in a corridor from Arlington
over the Potomac, for every carried flame

the name of a dead soldier: an element
fragile as ego, frightening as parturition,
necessary and intractable as dreaming.

The lapped, wheelborne integument, layer
within layer, at the core a dream of
something precious, ripped: Where are we?

The sleepers groan, stir, rewrap themselves
about the self's imponderable substance,
or clamber down, numb-footed, half in a drowse

of freezing dark, through a Stonehenge
of fuel pumps, the bison hulks slantwise
beside them, drinking. What is real except

what's fabricated? The jellies glitter
cream-capped in the cafeteria showcase;
gumball globes, Life Savers cinctured

in parcel gilt, plop from their housings
perfect, like miracles. Comb, nail clipper,
lip rouge, mirrors and emollients embody,

niched into the washroom wall case,
the pristine seductiveness of money.
Absently, without inhabitants, this

nowhere oasis wears the place name
of Indian Meadows. The westward-trekking
transhumance, once only, of a people who,

in losing everything they had, lost even
the names they went by, stumbling past
like caribou, perhaps camped here. Who

can assign a trade-in value to that sorrow?
The monk in sheepskin over tucked-up saffron
intoning to a drum becomes the metronome

of one more straggle up Pennsylvania Avenue
in falling snow, a whirl of tenderly
remorseless corpuscles, street gangs

amok among magnolias' pregnant wands,
a stillness at the heart of so much whirling:
beyond the torn integument of childbirth,

sometimes, wrapped like a papoose into a grief
not merely of the ego, you rediscover almost
the rest-in-peace of the placental coracle.

    2

Of what the dead were, living, one knows
so little as barely to recognize
the fabric of the backward-ramifying

antecedents, half-noted presences
in darkened rooms: the old, the feared,
the hallowed. Never the same river

drowns the unalterable doorsill. An effigy
in olive wood or pear wood, dank
with the sweat of age, walled in the dark

at Brauron, Argos, Samos: even the unwed
Athene, who had no mother, born—it's declared—
of some man's brain like every other pure idea,

had her own wizened cult object, kept
out of sight like the incontinent whimperer
in the backstairs bedroom, where no child

ever goes—to whom, year after year,
the fair linen of the sacred peplos
was brought in ceremonial procession—

flutes and stringed instruments, wildflower-
hung cattle, nubile Athenian girls, young men
praised for the beauty of their bodies. Who

can unpeel the layers of that seasonal
returning to the dark where memory fails,
as birds re-enter the ancestral flyway?

Daylight, snow falling, knotting of gears:
Chicago. Soot, the rotting backsides
of tenements, grimed trollshapes of ice

underneath the bridges, the tunnel heaving
like a birth canal. Disgorged, the infant
howling in the restroom; steam-table cereal,

pale coffee; wall-eyed TV receivers, armchairs
of molded plastic: the squalor of the day
resumed, the orphaned litter taken up again

unloved, the spawn of botched intentions,
grief a mere hardening of the gut,
a set piece of what can't be avoided:

parents by the tens of thousands living
unthanked, unpaid but in the sour coin
of resentment. Midmorning gray as zinc

along Route 80, corn-stubble quilting
the underside of snowdrifts, the cadaverous
belvedere of windmills, the sullen stare

of feedlot cattle; black creeks puncturing
white terrain, the frozen bottomland
a mush of willow tops; dragnetted in ice,

the Mississippi. Westward toward the dark,
the undertow of scenes come back to, fright
riddling the structures of interior history:

Where is it? Where, in the shucked-off
bundle, the hampered obscurity that has been
for centuries the mumbling lot of women,

did the thread of fire, too frail
ever to discover what it meant, to risk
even the taking of a shape, relinquish

the seed of possibility, unguessed-at
as a dream of something precious? Memory,
that exquisite blunderer, stumbling

like a migrant bird that finds the flyway
it hardly knew it knew except by instinct,
down the long-unentered nave of childhood,

late on a midwinter afternoon, alone
among the snow-hung hollows of the windbreak
on the far side of the orchard, encounters

sheltering among the evergreens, a small
stilled bird, its cap of clear yellow
slit by a thread of scarlet—the untouched

nucleus of fire, the lost connection
hallowing the wizened effigy, the mother
curtained in Intensive Care: a Candlemas

of moving lights along Route 80, at nightfall,
in falling snow, the stillness and the sorrow
of things moving back to where they came from.

TIMES SQUARE WATER MUSIC

By way of a leak
in the brickwork
beside a stairway
in the Times Square
subway, midway
between the IR
and the BM T, weeks
of sneaking seepage
had smuggled in,
that morning,
a centimeter
of standing water.

To ward off the herd
we tend to turn into,
turned loose on
the tiered terrain
of the Times Square
subway, somebody
had tried, with
a half-hearted
barricade or tether
of twine,
to cordon off
the stairway—

as though anyone
could tie up seepage
into a package—
down which the
water, a dripping
escapee, was surrep-
titiously proceeding
with the intent,
albeit inadvertent,
in time, at an
inferior level,
to make a lake.

Having gone round
the pond thus far
accumulated, bound
for the third, infra-
infernal hollow
of the underground,
where the N, RR,
and QB cars are
wont to travel,
in mid-descent I
stopped, abruptly way-
laid by a sound.

Alongside the iron-
runged nethermost
stairway, under
the banister,
a hurrying skein
of moisture had begun,
on its way down,
to unravel
into the trickle
of a musical
minuscule
waterfall.

Think of spleen-
wort, of moss
and maiden-
hair fernwork,
think of water
pipits, of ouzels
and wagtails
dipping into
the course of it
as the music
of it oozes
from the walls!

Think of it
undermining
the computer's
cheep, the time
clock's hiccup,
the tectonic
inchings of it
toward some
general crackup!
Think of it, think of
water running, running,
running till it
                    falls!

SALVAGE

Daily the cortege of crumpled
defunct cars
goes by by the lasagna-
layered flatbed
truckload: hardtop

reverting to tar smudge,
wax shine antiqued to crusted
winepress smear,
windshield battered to
intact ice-tint, a rarity

fresh from the Pleistocene.
I like it; privately
I find esthetic
satisfaction in these
ceremonial removals

from the category of
received ideas
to regions where pigeons'
svelte smoke-velvet
limousines, taxiing

in whirligigs, reclaim
a parking lot,
and the bag-laden
hermit woman, disencumbered
of a greater incubus,

the crush of unexamined
attitudes, stoutly
follows her routine,
mining the mountainsides
of our daily refuse

for artifacts: subversive
re-establishing
with each arcane
trash-basket dig
the pleasures of the ruined.

THE CORMORANT IN ITS ELEMENT

That bony potbellied arrow, wing-pumping along
implacably, with a ramrod's rigid adherence,
airborne, to the horizontal, discloses talents
one would never have guessed at. Plummeting

waterward, big black feet splayed for a landing
gear, slim head turning and turning, vermilion-
strapped, this way and that, with a lightning glance
over the shoulder, the cormorant astounding-

ly, in one sleek involuted arabesque, a vertical
turn on a dime, goes into that inimitable
vanishing-and-emerging-from-under-the-briny-

deep act which, unlike the works of Homo Houdini,
is performed for reasons having nothing at all
to do with ego, guilt, ambition, or even money.

CAMOUFLAGE

For Jo and Roy Shaw

It seemed at first like a piece of luck,
the discovery, there in the driveway,
of an odd sort of four-leaf clover—
no bankful of three-penny greenery
but a worried, hovering, wing-dragging
      killdeer's treasury—

a mosaic of four lopsided olives
or marbles you had to hunt
to find again every time, set into
the gravel as if by accident.
We'd have turned that bird's
      entire environment

upside down to have preserved them.
But what was there, after all,
we could have told her about foxes,
coons, cats, or the vandal
with its eye out for whatever anyone
      considers special?

In her bones, in her genes, in
the secret code of her behavior,
she already knew more than all our
bumbling daydreams, our palaver
about safeguards, could muster
      the wit to decipher:

how her whereabouts could vanish
into the gravel, how that brilliant
double-looped necklace could amputate
into invisibility the chevroned
cinnamon of her plumage. Cleverer
      than any mere learned,

merely devious equivocation,
that broken-wing pageant—
who taught her that? We have

no answer except accident,
the trillion-times-over-again
        repeated predicament

sifted with so spendthrift
a disregard for casualties
we can hardly bear to think of
a system so heartless, so shiftless
as being in charge here. It's
        too much like us—

except, after having looked so close
and so long at that casual handful
of dice, squiggle-spotted by luck
that made them half invisible,
watching too often the waltzing swoop
        of the bird's arrival

had meant a disruption of more usual
habits. For all our reading in the papers
about blunderers and risk-takers with
the shrug of nothing-much-matters-
how-those-things-turn-out, we'd unlearned
        to be good losers.

Sorrow, so far as we know, is not
part of a shorebird's equipment.
Nor is memory, of either survival
or losing, after the event.
Having squandered our attention, we
        were less prudent.

For a day, we couldn't quite afford
that morning's black discovery.
Grief is like money: there is only
so much of it we can give away.
        And that much grief, for a day,
                bankrupted our economy.

THE KINGFISHER

In a year the nightingales were said to be so loud
they drowned out slumber, and peafowl strolled screaming
beside the ruined nunnery, through the long evening
of a dazzled pub crawl, the halcyon color, portholed
by those eye-spots' stunning tapestry, unsettled
the pastoral nightfall with amazements opening.

Months later, intermission in a pub on Fifty-fifth Street
found one of them still breathless, the other quizzical,
acting the philistine, puncturing Stravinsky—"Tell
me, what *was* that racket in the orchestra about?"—
hauling down the Firebird, harum-scarum, like a kite,
a burnished, breathing wreck that didn't hurt at all.

Among the Bronx Zoo's exiled jungle fowl, they heard
through headphones of a separating panic, the bellbird
reiterate its single *chong*, a scream nobody answered.
When he mourned, "The poetry is gone," she quailed,
seeing how his hands shook, sobered into feeling old.
By midnight, yet another fifth would have been killed.

A Sunday morning, the November of their cataclysm
(Dylan Thomas brought in *in extremis* to St. Vincent's,
that same week, a symptomatic datum) found them
wandering a downtown churchyard. Among its headstones,
while from unruined choirs the noise of Christendom
poured over Wall Street, a benison in vestments,

a late thrush paused, in transit from some grizzled
spruce bog to the humid equatorial fireside: berry-
eyed, bark-brown above, with dark hints of trauma
in the stigmata of its underparts—or so, too bruised
just then to have invented anything so fancy,
later, re-embroidering a retrospect, she had supposed.

In gray England, years of muted recrimination (then
dead silence) later, she could not have said how many

spoiled takeoffs, how many entanglements gone sodden,
how many gaudy evenings made frantic by just one
insomniac nightingale, how many liaisons gone down
screaming in a stroll beside the ruined nunnery;

a kingfisher's burnished plunge, the color
of felicity afire, came glancing like an arrow
through landscapes of untended memory: ardor
illuminating with its terrifying currency
now no mere glimpse, no porthole vista
but, down on down, the uninhabitable sorrow.

EXMOOR

Lost aboard the roll of Kodac-
olor that was to have super-
seded all need to remember
Somerset were: a large flock

of winter-bedcover-thick-
pelted sheep up on the moor;
a stile, a church spire,
and an excess, at Porlock,

of tenderly barbarous antique
thatch in tandem with flower-
beds, relentlessly pictur-
esque, along every sidewalk;

a millwheel; and a millbrook
running down brown as beer.
Exempt from the disaster,
however, as either too quick

or too subtle to put on rec-
ord, were these: the flutter
of, beside that brown water,
with a butterfly-like flick

of fan-wings, a bright black-
and-yellow wagtail; at Dulver-
ton on the moor, the flavor
of the hot toasted teacake

drowning in melted butter
we had along with a bus-tour-
load of old people; the driver

's way of smothering every *r*
in the wool of a West Countr-
y diphthong, and as a Somer-

set man, the warmth he had for
the high, wild, heather-
dank wold he drove us over.

SUNDAY MUSIC

The Baroque sewing machine of Georg Friedrich
going back, going back to stitch back together
scraps of a scheme that's outmoded, all
those lopsidedly overblown expectations
now severely in need of revision, re
the nature of things, or more precisely
(back a stitch, back a stitch) the
nature of going forward.

No longer footpath-perpendicular, a monody
tootled on antelope bone, no longer
wheelbarrow heave-ho, the nature of going
forward is not perspective, not stairways,
not, as for the muse of Josquin or Gesualdo,
sostenuto, a leaning together
in memory of, things held onto
fusing and converging,

nor is it any longer an orbit, tonality's
fox-and-goose footprints going round
and round in the snow, the centripetal
force of the dominant. The nature of next
is not what we seem to be hearing
or imagine we feel; is not dance,
is not melody, not elegy,
is not even chemistry,

not Mozart leaching out seraphs
from a sieve of misfortune. The nature
of next is not fugue or rondo, not footpath
or wheelbarrow track, not steamships'
bass vibrations, but less and less
knowing what to expect, it's
the rate of historical
change going faster

and faster: it's noise, it's droids' stone-
deaf intergalactic twitter, it's get ready
to disconnect!—no matter how filled
our heads are with backed-up old
tunes, with polyphony, with basso
profundo fioritura, with this Concerto
Grosso's delectable (back a stitch,
back a stitch) Allegro.

BEETHOVEN, OPUS 111

For Norman Carey

*There are epochs . . . when mankind, not content with the pres-
ent, longing for time's deeper layers, like the plowman, thirsts
for the virgin soil of time.*

OSIP MANDELSTAM

—Or, conversely, hungers
for the levitations of the concert hall:
the hands like rafts of *putti*
out of a region where the dolorous stars
are fixed in glassy cerements of Art;
the *ancien régime*'s diaphanous plash
athwart the mounting throb of hobnails—
shod squadrons of vibration
mining the air, its struck ores hardening
into a plowshare, a downward wandering
disrupting every formal symmetry:
from the supine harp-case, the strung-foot
tendons under the mahogany, the bulldozer
in the bass unearths a Piranesian
catacomb: Beethoven ventilating,
with a sound he cannot hear, the cave-in
of recurring rage.
                              In the tornado country
of mid-America, my father
might have been his twin—a farmer
hacking at sourdock, at the strangle-
roots of thistles and wild morning glories,
setting out rashly, one October,
to rid the fencerows of poison ivy:
livid seed-globs turreted
in trinities of glitter, ripe
with the malefic glee no farmer doubts
lives deep down things. My father
was naïve enough—by nature
revolutionary, though he'd have
disowned the label—to suppose he might

in some way, minor but radical, disrupt
the givens of existence: set
his neighbors' thinking straight, undo
the stranglehold of reasons nations
send their boys off to war. That fall,
after the oily fireworks had cooled down
to trellises of hairy wicks,
he dug them up, rootstocks and all,
and burned them. Do-gooder!
The well-meant holocaust became
a mist of venom, sowing itself along
the sculptured hollows of his overalls,
braceleting wrists and collarbone—
a mesh of blisters spreading to a shirt
worn like a curse. For weeks
he writhed inside it. Awful.

                         High art
with a stiff neck: an upright Steinway
bought in Chicago; a chromo of a Hobbema
tree-avenue, or of Millet's imagined peasant,
the lark she listens to invisible, perhaps
irrelevant: harpstrings and fripperies of air
congealed into an object nailed against the wall,
its sole ironic function (if it has any)
to demonstrate that one, though he may
grunt and sweat at work, is not a clod.
Beethoven might declare the air
his domicile, the winds kin, the tornado
a kind of second cousin; here,
his labor merely shimmers—a deracinated
album leaf, a bagatelle, the "Moonlight"
rendered with a dying fall (the chords
subside, disintegrate, regroup
in climbing sequences *con brio*); there's
no dwelling on the sweet past here,
there being no past to speak of
other than the setbacks: typhoid

in the wells, half the first settlers
dead of it before a year was out;
diphtheria and scarlet fever
every winter; drought, the Depression,
a mortgage on the mortgage. High art
as a susurrus, the silk and perfume
of unsullied hands. Those hands!—
driving the impressionable wild with anguish
for another life entirely: the Lyceum circuit,
the doomed diving bell of Art.
                              Beethoven
in his workroom: ear trumpet,
conversation book and pencil, candlestick,
broken crockery, the Graf piano
wrecked by repeated efforts to hear himself—
out of a humdrum squalor the levitations,
the shakes and triplets, the *Adagio*
molto semplice e cantabile, the Arietta
a disintegrating surf of blossom
opening along the keyboard, along the fencerows
the astonishment of sweetness. My father,
driving somewhere in Kansas or Colorado,
in dustbowl country, stopped the car
to dig up by the roots a flower
he'd never seen before—a kind
of prickly poppy most likely, its luminousness
wounding the blank plains like desire.
He mentioned in a letter the disappointment
of his having hoped it might transplant—
an episode that brings me near tears,
still, as even his dying does not—
that awful dying, months-long, hunkered,
irascible. From a clod no plowshare
could deliver, a groan for someone
(because he didn't want to look
at anything) to take away the flowers,
a bawling as of slaughterhouses, slogans

of a general uprising: *Freiheit!*
Beethoven, shut up with the four walls
of his deafness, rehearsing the unhearable
semplice e cantabile, somehow reconstituting
the blister shirt of the intolerable
into these shakes and triplets, a hurrying
into flowering along the fencerows: dying,
for my father, came to be like that
finally—in its messages the levitation
of serenity, as though the spirit might
aspire, in its last act,

                    to walk on air.

THE WOODLOT

Clumped murmuring above a sump of loam—
grass-rich, wood-poor—that first the plow,
then the inventor (his name plowed under
somewhere in the Patent Office) of barbed wire,
taught, if not fine manners, how at least to follow
the surveyor's rule, the woodlot nodes of willow,
evergreen or silver maple gave the prairie grid
what little personality it had.
                         Who could
have learned fine manners where the air,
that rude nomad, still domineered,
without a shape it chose to keep,
oblivious of section lines, in winter
whisking its wolfish spittle to a froth
that turned whole townships into
one white wallow? Barbed wire
kept in the cattle but would not abrade
the hide or draw the blood
of gales hurled gnashing like seawater over fences'
laddered apertures, rigging the landscape
with the perspective of a shipwreck. Land-chained,
the blizzard paused to caterwaul
at every windbreak, a rage the worse
because it was in no way personal.
                         Against
the involuted tantrums of spring and summer—
sackfuls of ire, the frightful udder
of the dropped mammocumulus
become all mouth, a lamprey
swigging up whole farmsteads, suction
dislodging treetrunks like a rotten tooth—
luck and a cellarhole were all
a prairie dweller had to count on.
                         Whether
the inventor of barbed wire was lucky
finally in what he found himself
remembering, who knows? Did he

ever, even once, envision
the spread of what he'd done
across a continent: whale-song's
taut dulcimer still thrumming as it strung together
orchard, barnyard, bullpen, feedlot,
windbreak: wire to be clambered over,
crawled through or slid under, shepherded—
the heifers staring—to an enclosure
whose ceiling's silver-maple tops
stir overhead, uneasy, in the interminably
murmuring air? Deep in it, under
appletrees like figures in a ritual, violets
are thick, a blue cellarhole
of pure astonishment.
                          It is
the earliest memory. Before it,
I/you, whatever that conundrum may yet
prove to be, amounts to nothing.

IMAGO

Sometimes, she remembers, a chipped flint
would turn up in a furrow,
pink as a peony (from the iron in it)
or as the flared throat of a seashell:
a nomad's artifact fished from the broth,
half sea half land—hard evidence
of an unfathomed state of mind.

Nomads. The wagon train that camped
and left its name on Mormon Ridge.
The settlers who moved on to California,
bequeathing a laprobe pieced from the hide
of a dead buffalo, the frail sleigh
that sleeps under the haymow, and a headstone
so small it might be playing house,
for the infant daughter, aged two days,
no name, they also left behind.

Half sea half land: the shirker propped
above her book in a farmhouse parlor
lolls with the merfolk who revert to foam,
eyeing at a distance the lit pavilions
that seduced her, their tailed child,
into the palaces of metamorphosis. She pays
now (though they do not know this)
by treading, at every step she takes,
on a parterre of tomahawks.

A thirst for something definite so dense
it feels like drowning. Grant Wood
turned everything to cauliflower,
the rounded contours of a thunderhead,
flint-hard. He made us proud:
though all those edges might not be quite
the way it was, at least he'd tried.

"But it has no form!" they'd say to
the scribbler whose floundering fragments

kept getting out of hand—and who, either
fed up with or starved out of
her native sloughs, would, stowed aboard
the usual nomadic moving van, trundle her
dismantled sensibility elsewhere.

Europe, that hodgepodge of ancestral
calamities, was hard and handsome, its rubble
confident, not shriveling on the vine,
as here, like an infertile melon—the Virgin
jejune in her grotto of cold plaster, half sick
of that sidelong enclave, the whispered "Cathlick."

Antiquity unshrouds on wimpling canvas,
adjunct of schoolhouse make-believe: the Italy
of urns and cypresses, of stairways
evolving toward a state of mind
not to be found except backstage
among hunchbacks and the miscreants
who control the scenery, flanked
by a pair of masks whose look, at even
this remove, could drill through bone:
the tragic howl, the comic rictus,
eyeholes that stare out of the crypt
of what no grownup is ever heard to speak of
but in the strangled tone whose lexicon
is summed up in one word: *Bankrupt.*

Bankrupt: the abysm of history,
a slough to be pulled out of
any way you could. Antiquity, the backward
suction of the dark, amounted to a knothole
you plugged with straw, old rags, pages
ripped from last year's Sears Roebuck catalog,
anything, to ward off the blizzard.
Not so, for the born-again, the

shuddering orifices of summer.
On prayer-meeting night, outside
the vestibule among multiple
bell-pulls of Virginia creeper,
the terrible clepsydra of becoming
distils its drop: a luna moth, the emblem
of the born-again, furred like an orchid
behind the ferned antennae, a totem-
garden of lascivious pheromones,
hangs, its glimmering streamers
pierced by the dripstone burin of the eons
with the predatory stare out of the burrow,
those same eyeholes. Imago
of unfathomable evolvings, living
only to copulate and drop its litter,
does it know what it is, what it has been,
what it may or must become?

STACKING THE STRAW

In those days the oatfields'
fenced-in vats of running platinum,
the yellower alloy of wheat and barley,
whose end, however gorgeous all that trammeled
rippling in the wind, came down
to toaster-fodder, cereal
as a commodity, were a rebuke
to permanence—to bronze or any metal
less utilitarian than the barbed braids
that marked off a farmer's property,
or the stoked dinosaur of a steam engine
that made its rounds from farm to farm,
after the grain was cut and bundled,
and powered the machine that did the threshing.

Strawstacks' beveled loaves, a shape
that's now extinct, in those days were
the nearest thing the region had
to monumental sculpture. While hayracks
and wagons came and went, delivering bundles,
carting the winnowed ore off to the granary,

a lone man with a pitchfork stood aloft
beside the hot mouth of the blower,
building about himself, forkful
by delicately maneuvered forkful,
a kind of mountain, the golden
stuff of mulch, bedding for animals.
I always thought of him with awe—

a craftsman whose evolving altitude
gave him the aura of a hero. He'd come down
from the summit of the season's effort
black with the baser residues of that
discarded gold. Saint Thomas of Aquino
also came down from the summit
of a lifetime's effort, and declared
that everything he'd ever done was straw.

PALM SUNDAY

Neither the wild tulip, poignant
and sanguinary, nor the dandelion
blowsily unbuttoning, answers
the gardener's imperative, if need be,
to maim and hamper in the name of order,
or the taste for rendering adorable
the torturer's implements—never mind
what entrails, not yet trampled under
by the feet of choirboys (sing,
my tongue, the glorious battle),
mulch the olive groves, the flowering
of apple and almond, the boxwood
corridor, the churchyard yew,
the gallows tree.

REMEMBERING GREECE

For Peter Kybart

At noon in this blue cove of the Atlantic
a stiff breeze gets up, exactly as you've seen
it do off Delos. Poseidon, to whose unease
mumbling Delphi purported to assign some meaning,

is quiescent here. Snoring under northern shores,
the Earth-Disturber has hardly more than whimpered
since, enrobed in thickening catastrophes of ice,
the drowned once-mountaintops of this red granite

all but suffocated in his bath—today so blue,
it halfway dislocates itself to the Aegean
and becomes, if only in the way events can weigh
upon events, the bloodied bath of Agamemnon.

RAIN AT BELLAGIO

For Doris Thompson Myers

I

The omnipresence of the sound of water: rain
on the graveled walks, the lakeside terraces,
the red pantiles of Bellagio.

At Paestum we had not heard it.
An acreage of thyme, winnowed by sea breezes.
A line of blue out past the silted harbor—
unauthenticated because unheard,
a scene one might have dreamed.

At Herculaneum, a stoppage of the ears.
Cicadas mute, an oleander stillness.
Rancor of cypresses. Impacted fire.
Effete ribaldry strangling in hot mud
up to the nostrils. Water stricken
from the ledgers of memory.

At Naples, human noise inundating the bayfront,
lapping at castles' elephantine hooves, rampaging
tenement ravines. Once in the night
I woke and knew it had been raining—
not from the sound but from the smell, as though
an animal had left its spoor.

Under an aspect less clement, the trickle
of sewers, the vine-patched bombholes,
bambini with no underpants, gnarled women
wearing the black of perpetual resignation,
might have figured more gravely than as a condiment,
garlic for a week of living well.

2

Aboard the *wagons-lits* we drank Est! Est! Est!,
leaned tipsily out of windows, behaved

as though we owned the railway car, owned
the platform as it receded, owned even, overhead,
the diminution to a half-perceived scintilla
of the stars, after the manner of the young who travel
Europe, garnering experience in pairs.

We passed the Apennines asleep, and woke in a country
where the color of the olive trees was rainy.
Gray rain muddying the emerald of ricefields,
blurring, across the flood plain of the Po, the vague
geometry of poplars on the march—a part
of some interminable uprising.

At Milan a drizzle, the boulevards inlaid
with dun-colored patines, the slough of plane trees.
A car sent from the villa, behind whose steamed windows
we talk as freely as though the driver had no ears.
Glimpsing, through sheets of rain, the first gray-green,
narrow windings of Lake Como,
the red pantiles of Monza and Lecco,
the little farms, the villa walls
sequestering unimagined pleasures. Vineyards.
Terraces. The starred darkness of lemon trees
through the downpour. Gravel under our shoes,
a footman holding an umbrella. All as in
that terrifying place where no one is admitted
whose taste is not impeccable.

3

Servants. The butler's practiced deference,
the liquid glance unerring as a falcon's—
a lisp in the shrubbery, a blur of wingbars
and he's placed you. On the hall table
tuberoses' opening racemes purport a sadness
the equal of Elysium. Massed carnations
in a cushioned bedroom, a bath overlooking

the flutter of chaffinches, cypresses'
columned melancholy, the lacquered foliage
of magnolias seen from the balcony, are no refuge
from the surveillance of chambermaids, scathing
as a penitent's examination of conscience.
The scuffed suitcase cannot escape: as soon as
your back is turned, they have
already unpacked it.

Out on the lake a white traghetto, moving
almost without pause from one shore to the other,
a punctual amphibious spider, skeins
into one zigzag the descending
clatter from the campaniles of Bellagio,
of Varenna and Cadenabbia, as though reining
the fragments of experience into one process—
being-and-becoming fused, a single scheme.

The rustle of descending silk (these shores
being mulberry country), the curtains drawn
against the prerogative of the chambermaids,
behind closed doors, having had our tea,
conspiratorially, two high-church Episcopalians, we begin
to read aloud the office of Compline.

The damask weave of luxury, the arras
of melodrama. A wailing about the eaves.
Confidences wading like a salvage operation
toward an untidy past: the admirer
who had in fact been a bricklayer,
who wore dirty undershirts; the rue
of not-yet-dealt-with gaffes, chagrins
and false positions, tinder
for the scorn of maître d's, the pained
look of a host whose taste is impeccable:
hazards of a murderous civility, the beast
snared in a nightmare of living well.

4

Cocktails in the salotto, underneath a portrait
of the late owner, a distiller's heiress
of dim but cultivated beauty, whose third spouse
left her title to an extinct principality. The villa,
acquired by caprice, became her favorite household.
Though in the way of moral character not much
is to be expected, *noblesse oblige:* the servants—
eighty of them altogether—must be provided for.
Emissaries of those foundations into which
the larger fortunes have unavoidably been siphoned
were circuitously whispered to; and so, the times
being what they have become, the princeliest
of the seventeen bedrooms, stripped
of its cushier urgings to dalliance,
is now a conference room—this week
for a conclave of jurisprudes, the week after
for experts in the field of public health
concerning the eradication of malaria.

Reclamation of the land: the labor gangs,
the overseers, the seasonal migrations,
the Lombard plain at last made habitable,
a source of fortunes: irrigated water meadows,
ricefields, wheat, mulberries, the channeled music
of the Po, the Oglio, the Adda, the Ticino. Vineyards.
Landed estates. Walled properties above Lake Como,
for the view. A rural proletariat whose fortunes
and miseries go unrecorded.

5

In her declining years the Principessa
was to be seen leaning, as she made her rounds
nuzzled in sable against the lake damp,
on the arm of her butler.

The indispensable tyranny of servants.
Gardeners, kitchen maids, woodcutters, grooms,
footmen. Private secretaries.
Confessors. Archbishops.
Above the fever trap of the Maremma
the ritual complicity: in castle towers
the secret stair, the cached aconite,
the hired assassin.

Fiefdoms. Latifundia. The wealth of nations.
The widening distance between rich and poor,
between one branch and another of the tree of misery.
A view of lakeside terraces
to sell one's soul for.

6

Among the company at dinner, Professor B.,
reputedly the best mind in Italy,
who speaks no English; also Professor d'E.,
who speaks it more exquisitely than any native—
slim, fair, elfin, author of a legal treatise
no one (he says) has read.
     —Then I will read it.
     —Oh, but really it is very dull.
The weather in Italy, he says, is changing.
Now that charcoal is no longer burned
extensively, the forests have grown up again,
forests draw moisture—*Ecco!*

Flooding along the Po, the Adige, the Ticino.
Dykes giving way at Ferrara, inundations
at Rimini, the beetfields of Ravenna
already under water. On the flood plain,
the mosaics of Sant' Apollinare in Classe
ripple as though drowned—redemption
envisioned as a wall of water.

7

What does a place like this not offer?
Flawless cuisine, a first-rate cellar,
mountain footpaths laced with wild cyclamen
and maidenhair; topiary, sunken gardens,
wood nymphs and a dying slave in marble; even,
when nothing short of total solitude
will do, a hermitage.

My friend is twenty,
blond as Lucrezia Borgia, her inclinations
nurtured with care since childhood.
She speaks three languages and has had
six proposals. Since January
her existence has been an exercise
in living like a Principessa. Her father
still cannot fathom what has happened.
He points, appealing, to a letter
on the hall table, overhung
by the tuberoses' extravagant love-death,
addressed to an abbess.

And will she be free to leave if she should wish to?
He, for one, does not believe it. They will wear her down
in that enclosed community, those Anglican Benedictines.
She will become nothing other than a model prisoner.
That, as he understands it, is the long and short
of what what they call *formation* amounts to.

One might have said by way of a response (but did not)
that living under vows, affianced to a higher poverty,
might likewise be an exercise in living well.

8

Her last evening amounts to an exercise in prevarication.
Where precisely she is going, and why, she has

given up explaining. Dinner is a banquet. Afterward,
half sozzled on red wine followed by champagne
followed by Strega, we're in raincoats,
climbing into a villa car with a pair
of half-fledged jurisprudes. A halt
somewhere along the way, the rain slackening
and closing in again like trees in a landscape,
to snitch grapes from a vineyard. We arrive
at the farewell party pretending we're bacchantes.

Antique U.S. jazz on a portable phonograph.
Liqueurs. Chocolates. My friend dancing
the cha-cha-cha, engaging in mock flirtations
with a moody Italian, then with a cheerful one
whose profession entails the proliferation of supermarkets.
      —But how *can* you?
      —And why isn't what's good for your country
         good also for Italy?

A prolonged huddle with the cheerful one. Emerging,
they announce they have an announcement:
they have decided to get married
for about a week. At midnight,
trying for a departure, we find the door
locked against us, the key hidden prettily
in somebody's décolletage. Everybody
is going away tomorrow. We say goodbye
to the jurisprudes, the young footman
standing expressionless beside the door.

    9

The pang of bells, through rain-filled dark,
at every hour. Half slumber,
feeble morning light. At seven, booted
and raincoated, we're plunging through the wet
to board the traghetto—the only passengers,

along with a truckload of Italian beer—for Cadenabbia
and early communion at the English church.

A port, a buoy, a rudder: hymnbook similes
capsize in the act of kneeling
and receiving the substance of such controversy,
cataclysms from the winepress of the glaciers,
whatever it is that knows itself only
in the sense of being carried,
all the bridges out, surrounded
by the rush of moving water—total
self-abandonment perceived as living well.

A rush for the landing, the water rushing alongside,
down gutters, over cobblestones. In one hour
the level of the lake has risen astoundingly.
Aboard the traghetto, a priest
wears a violet-lined biretta
and buckles on his shoes.

Seeing how the picturesque outlives its meaning.

10

Punctually at three in the afternoon, our luggage
waits by the door, the car stands in the rain,
its motor running. Bathos of tuberoses
on the hall table, the butler's formal bow,
the footman holding an umbrella. Gravel
under our shoes. Behind the steamed windows
confidences interspersed with silences.
At Milan, dim through fatigue, a watershed:
for the rest of our lives, we will be traveling
in opposite directions. Behind us, limestone
and chestnut mountainsides, streaming, release
their increment of moisture: rain, glacier melt,
the wine of change. Ahead of us,

spilling across the lap of Italy, the tributaries
of the Po—the Adda, the Oglio, the Sesia—
mingle and descend toward Ferrara,
toward Rimini and Ravenna: uncontrollable
as rumor, as armies set in motion,
the sound of water.

11

Sometimes since, in dreams I find myself obliged
to assume, without previous instruction, control
of a plane I have no memory of boarding. I wake
without ever having learned the outcome. Or,
in another region, I find myself
face to face with the transparent strata
of experience, the increment of years,
as a wall of inundation, the drowned mosaic
glimmering above the flood plain. Waking,
I hear the night sounds merge, a single rustle
as of silk, as though becoming might amend,
unbroken, to one stilled, enclosing skein.

12

At the Abbey, between the shored-up Norman church
and the trefoiled oak of the pilgrim hostel,
running liquid and garrulous through a life of silence,
cushioned and tended between banks of tamed wildflowers,
the sound of water: indivisible, unstilled,
unportioned by the bells that strike the hours.

OR CONSIDER PROMETHEUS

*In 1859 petroleum was discovered in Pennsylvania. Kerosene,
petroleum, and paraffin began rapidly to replace whale oil,
sperm oil, and spermaceti wax. . . . Consider whaling as*
FRONTIER, *and* INDUSTRY. *A product wanted, men got it:
big business. The Pacific as sweatshop . . . the whaleship as
factory, the whaleboat the precision instrument. . . .*
CHARLES OLSON, *Call Me Ishmael*

I

Would Prometheus, cursing on his rock
as he considered fire, the smuggled gem
inside the weed stem, and the excesses
since his protracted punishment began,

have cursed the ocean's copious antidote,
its lapping, cold, incessant undulance
plowed to shards by wheeling porpoises,
hydrogen-cum-oxygen fanned up in mimicries

of hard carbon, diamond of purest water,
the unforbidden element crosscut by fire,
its breakup the absolving smile of rainbows?
Or, considering leviathan, whose blameless

progenitors turned from the shore, from its
seducing orchards, renouncing the prehensile
dangle of a brain all eyes and claws,
twittering fishhook strategies of grasp

and mastery, for immersion among moving
declivities, have envied the passivity
whose massive ease is no more than his own
tormented rectitude, immune from drowning?

2

How would the great cetaceans, Houyhnhnm
intelligences sans limbs, ungoaded by

the Promethean monkeyshines that gave us
haute cuisine, autos-da-fé and fireworks,

dining al fresco off cuttlefish and krill,
serving up baleen-strained plankton, whose
unmanipulative ears explore Olympian parterres
of sonar, devise the ringing calculus

of icebergs, compute the density of ships
as pure experience of hearing—how
would these basking reservoirs of fuel,
wax and glycerine have read the trypots

readied for their rendering into tallow
for a thousand candles? How, astronomers
of the invisible, would they have tracked
the roaring nimbus of that thieving

appetite, our hunger for the sun, or
charted the harrowing of jet and piston
pterodactyls, robots fed on their successor,
fire-drinking vampires of hydrocarbon?

LETTERS FROM JERUSALEM

Engines of burning took him there
and brought back the first postcard,
a view of Jerusalem. The high air
swam with domes, their drowned gilding
glimmering like live fish scales.
The sky at night was an aquarium
of light-years whose distances
at noon, converging, turned the desert
           to burning glass.

The kibbutzim aren't quite, he admits,
what he'd expected. The Talmud
couldn't care less about anybody's
happiness. But is that (he writes)
even important? Perhaps the true
arrival is always inward? He walks
the hills, the clogged bazaars,
everywhere. He is learning Hebrew.
           Immerse, immerse—

inward but also downward. He sees
time impend, the weather changing.
Clouds mass on the horizon; daylight
shrinks backward to the Maccabees'
last reckoning. In secret, from
the squalid rigor of the Yeshiva
and his unheated room, he flees
with Saint-Exupéry into regions
           of wind, sand and stars.

Immersion, thirst for roots, the passion
of expecting less: he asks now (he writes)
no more than to be here as a witness.
He begins even to dream in Hebrew:
locutions bend as though half in,
half out of water. But the watershed

that waits is made of fire: a cherub
in the doorway poses the blazing
        conundrum of the Jews

whose Biblical injunction is: if he stays
he must go into the army. The 'sixties
subversive pacifist he was must unadopt
that arrogance or lose Jerusalem.
A bush burned once; volcanoes
tutored the patriarchs; Elijah
was taken up in rafts of flame.
From Moscow, rumors arrive of new
        pogroms. He stays.

The latest letter, with no date, begins
Shalom! Tomorrow his leave ends,
then back to the desert. Tanks are less
accommodating even than the Talmud
to a divided mind. The promised land
more and more is dense with engines.
Converging overhead, in skies that swam,
the distances grow predatory and explode
        with burning seraphim.

BERCEUSE

Listen to Gieseking playing a berceuse
of Chopin—the mothwing flutter
light as ash, perishable as burnt paper—

and sleep, now the furnaces of Auschwitz
are all out, and tourists go there.
The purest art has slept with turpitude,

we all pay taxes. Sleep. The day of waking
waits, cloned from the phoenix—
a thousand replicas in upright silos,

nurseries of the ultimate enterprise.
Decay will undo what it can, the rotten
fabric of our repose connives with doomsday.

Sleep on, scathed felicity. Sleep, rare
and perishable relic. Imagining's no shutter
against the absolute, incorrigible sunrise.

THE DAHLIA GARDENS

There are places no history can reach.
NORMAN MAILER,
The Armies of the Night

Outside the river entrance, between the Potomac
and the curbed flowerbeds, a man walks up and down,
has been walking this last half hour. November leaves
skip in the wind or are lifted, unresisting,
to mesh with the spent residue of dahlias'
late-summer blood and flame, leached marigolds,
knives of gladioli flailed to ribbons:
parts of a system that seems, on the face of it,
to be all waste, entropy, dismemberment;
but which perhaps, given time enough, will prove
to have refused nothing tangible,
                                    enjambed
without audible clash, with no more than a whiplash
incident, to its counterpart, a system
shod in concrete, cushioned in butyl, riding
chariots of thermodynamics, adept with the unrandom,
the calculus of lifting and carrying, with vectors,
clocks, chronicles, calibrations.
                                    File clerks
debouch into the dusk—it is rush hour; headlights
thicken, a viscous chain along the Potomac—
from concentric corridors, five sides
within five sides, grove leading on to grove
lit by autonomous purrings, daylight
on demand, dense with the pristine,
the dead-white foliage of those archives
that define and redefine with such precision,
such subtleties of exactitude, that only
the honed mind's secret eye can verify
or vouch for its existence, how the random
is to be overcome, the unwelcome
forestalled, the arcane calamity
at once refused, delineated and dwelt on. Where,

as here, triune Precaution, Accumulation
and Magnitude obtain, such levitations
and such malignities have come, with time,
to seem entirely natural—this congeries
being unquestionably the largest
office building in Christendom.
                            The man alone
between blackened flowerbeds and the blackening
Potomac moves with care, as though balanced
astride the whiplash between system and system—
wearing an overcoat, hatless, thinning-haired,
a man of seemingly mild demeanor
who might have been a file clerk
were it not for his habit of writing down
notes to himself on odd scraps of paper,
old bills, the backs of envelopes, or in a notebook
he generally forgets to bring with him,
and were it not for the wine jug
he carries (the guard outside the river entrance,
as he pauses, has observed it, momentarily puzzled)
cradled close against his overcoat.
                            By now file clerks,
secretaries, minor and major bureaucrats, emerging
massively through the several ports of egress,
along the ramps, past the walled flowerbeds,
which the lubrications and abrasions of routine,
the multiple claims of a vigilant anxiety,
the need for fine tuning, for continual
readjustment of expectation, have rendered
largely negligible, flow around him.
He moves against the flux, toward the gardens.
Around him, leaves skip in the wind
like a heartbeat, like a skipped
heartbeat

        if I were a dead leaf
        thou mightest bear

                             He shivers,
cradling the wine jug, his heart beating strangely;
his mind fills up with darkness

                overland, the inching caravans
                the blacked-out troop trains
                convoys through ruined villages
                along the Mekong

                              merging
with the hydrocarbon-dark, headlight-inflamed Potomac

                the little lights   the candles
                flickering on Christmas eve
                the one light left burning
                in a front hallway   kerosene-
                lit windows in the pitch dark
                of back-country roads

                              His mind
plunges like a derrick
into that pitch dark as he uncorks the wine jug
and with a quick gesture not unlike
a signing with the cross (but he is a Quaker)
begins the anointing of himself with its contents,
with the ostensible domestic Rhine wine
or chablis, which is not wine—which
in fact is gasoline

                tallow, rushlight, whale oil, coal oil,
                gas jet: black fat of the Ur-tortoise
                siphoned from stone, a shale-tissued
                carapace: hydrocarbon unearthed
                and peeled away, process by process,
                in stages not unlike the stages
                of revelation, to a gaseous plume
                that burns like a bush, a perpetual

dahlia of incandescence, midway
between Wilmington and Philadelphia
gaslight, and now these filamented
avenues, wastelands and windows
of illumination, gargoyles,
gasconades, buffooneries of neon,
stockpiled incendiary pineapples,
pomegranates of jellied gasoline
that run along the ground, that cling
in a blazing second skin
to the skins of children

Anointing the overcoat, and underneath it the pullover
with one elbow out, he sees, below the whiplash threshold,
darkness boil up, a vatful of sludge, a tar pit,
a motive force that is all noise: jet engines,
rush-hour aggressions, blast furnaces,
headline-grabbing self-importances

the urge to engineer events
compel a change of government,
a change of heart, a shift
in the wind's direction—lust
after mastery, manipulations
of the merely political

Hermaphrodite of pity and violence, the chambered
pistil and the sword-bearing archangel,
scapegoat and self-appointed avenger, contend,
embrace, are one. He strikes the match.
A tiger leap, a singing envelope goes up,
blue-wicked, a saffron overcoat of burning

in the forests of the night
make me thy lyre

                              Evolving
          out of passionless dismemberment,
          a nerveless parturition, green wheels'
          meshed intercalibration with the sun

A random leaf, seized by the updraft, shrivels
unresisting; fragments of black ash
drift toward the dahlia gardens

          from dim tropisms of avoidance,
          articulated, node upon internode,
          into a scream, the unseen filament
          that never ends, that runs
          through all our chronicles

          a manifesto flowering like a dahlia
          into whole gardens of astonishment—
          the sumptuous crimson,
          heart's dark, the piebald
          saffron and scarlet riding
          the dahlia gardens of
          the lake of Xochimilco:

          Benares, marigold-garlanded
          suttee, the burning ghats
          alongside the Ganges: at
          the An Quang pagoda, saffron
          robes charring in fiery
          transparency, a bath of burning

Scraps of charred paper, another kind of foliage,
drift toward the dahlia gardens

                         a leaf
                   thou mightest bear

                                    The extravaganza
of a man afire having seized, tigerlike, the attention
it now holds with the tenacity of napalm, of the homebound
file clerks, secretaries, minor and major bureaucrats,
superimposing upon multiple adjustments,
the fine tuning of Precaution and Accumulation,
the demands of Magnitude, what the concentric
groves of those archives have no vocabulary
for dwelling on, the uniformed man of action,
in whom precaution and the unerring impulse
are one, springs forward to pound and pummel,
extinguishing the manifesto as decently as possible.
                                                    Someone,
by now, has sent for an ambulance.

The headlights crawl, slowed by increasing density,
along the Potomac, along the diagonal thoroughfares,
along the freeways, toward Baltimore, toward Richmond,
toward Dulles and toward Friendship Airport, the airborne
engines' alternating red
and green, a pause and then again a red,
a green, a waking fantasy upborne
on a lagoon of hydrocarbon, as
the dahlia gardens ride the lake of Xochimilco.
While the voiceless processes of a system
that in the end perhaps will have
refused nothing tangible, continue neither
to own nor altogether to refuse the burning filament
that runs through all our chronicles, uniting
system with system into one terrible mandala,
the stripped hydrocarbon
burns like a bush, a gaseous plume
midway between Wilmington and Philadelphia.

THE BURNING CHILD

After a few hours' sleep, the father had a dream that his child was standing beside his bed, caught him by the arm and whispered reproachfully: "Father, don't you see I'm burning?"
                    FREUD, *The Interpretation of Dreams*

Dreamwork, the mnemonic flicker
of the wave of lost particulars—
whose dream, whose child, where, when, all lost
except the singed reprieve, its fossil ardor
burnished to a paradigm of grief,
half a century before the cattle cars,
the shunted parceling—*links, rechts*—
in a blaspheming parody of judgment
by the Lord of burning: the bush, the lava flow,
the chariot, the pillar. What is, even so,
whatever breathes but a reprieve, a risk,
a catwalk stroll between the tinder
and the nurture whose embrace is drowning?

The dream redacted cannot sleep; it whimpers
so relentlessly of lost particulars, I can't
help thinking of the dreamer as your father,
sent for by the doctors the night he said the *Sh'ma*
over the dim phoenix-nest of scars
you were, survivor
pulled from behind a blazing gas tank
that summer on the Cape, those many years
before we two, by a shuttlecock-and-battle-
dore, a dreamworklike accretion of nitwit
trouvées, were cozened into finding how
minute particulars might build themselves
into a house that almost looks substantial:
just as I think of how, years earlier,
the waves at Surfside on Nantucket, curveting
like herded colts, subsiding, turned
against my staggering thighs, a manacle
of iron cold I had to be pulled out of. Drowning,

since, has seemed a native region's ocean,
that anxiety whose further shores are lurid
with recurrences of burning.

The people herded from the cattle cars
first into barracks, then to killing chambers,
stripped of clothes, of names, of chattels—all those
of whom there would remain so few particulars:
I think of them, I think of how your mother's
people made the journey, and of how

                         unlike
    my own forebears who made the journey,
    when the rush was on, aboard a crowded
    train from Iowa to California, where,
    hedged by the Pacific's lunging barricades,
    they brought into the world the infant
    who would one day be my father, and
    (or the entire astonishment, for me, of
    having lived until this moment would
    have drowned unborn, unburied without
    ever having heard of Surfside) chose
    to return, were free to stay or go
    back home, go anywhere at all—

                         not one
outlived the trip whose terminus was burning.

The catwalk shadows of the cave, the whimper
of the burning child, the trapped
reprieve of nightmare between the
tinder and the nurture whose
embrace is drowning.

from WHAT THE LIGHT WAS LIKE

(1985)

THE AUGUST DARKS

Stealth of the flood tide, the moon dark
but still at work, the herring shoals
somewhere offshore, looked for
but not infallible, as the tide is,
as the August darks are—

stealth of the seep of daylight, the boats
bird-white above the inlet's altering
fish-silver, the murmur of the motor
as the first boat slips out
ahead of daylight

into the opening aorta, that heaving
reckoning whose flux informs the heart-
beat of the fisherman—poor,
dark, fallible-infallible
handful of a marvel

murmuring unasked inside the ribcage,
workplace covert as the August darks are,
as is the moon's work, masked within
the blazing atrium of daylight,
the margin of its dwindling

sanguine as with labor, but effortless:
as is the image, far out, illusory
at the dark's edge, of the cruise ship
moving, seemingly unscathed by effort,
bright as a stage set

for the miming of the tiara'd swan's danced
dying, the heartbeat's prodigies of strain
unseen, the tendons' ache, the blood-
stained toe shoes, the tulle
sweat-stained, contained

out where the herring wait, beyond
the surf-roar on the other side of silence
we should die of (George Eliot
declared) were we to hear it. Many
have already died of it.

LOW TIDE AT SCHOODIC

Force, just here, rolls up
pomaded into vast blue curls
fit for the Sun King, then crumples
to a stuff of ruffs and kerchiefs
over ruined doorposts, the rubble
of an overthrow no one remembers
except through cooled
extrapolation—tunnels
underneath the granite,
the simmering moat, the darkened sill
we walk on now,
prowling the planar windowpanes of tidepools
for glimpses of kelp's ribboned whips,
the dead men's fingers.
                              Boulders
smothered in a fur of barnacles
become a slum, a barrio
of hardened wigwams, each
(notwithstanding a seeming armor
that invites, when added to the fate
of being many, the hobnails
of a murderous indifference)
holding an entity no less
perishably tender than any
neonate delivered, red
and squalling, in the singular.
                              Spruces,
turreted above the ledge,
lodge in the downdraft
of their precarious stairwells
a warbler who, all nerves tuned to
alarums, dapper in a yellow domino,
a noose of dark about his throat,
appends his anxious signature—
a wiry wheeze,
a blurred flute note.

BERTIE GOES HUNTING

For Mary Jo Salter and Brad Leithauser

Dear beast, luxurious of pelt,
moon-orbed possessor of the
screen-door-unlatching paw,
the lurk that twitches in
    the haunch at every

piebald quiver of out-in-the-
open; past the fern-flanked
porchside boundary, a froth
of goldenrod and timothy
    absorbs his predatory

crouch-and-spring, quick-
silver underside of memory,
the lunge-evoking, paradisal
rustle of the underbrush, the
    just-missed quarry:

his vanishings into a history
so dense with molecules, so
chary of the traceable, you
never quite believe the ata-
    vism's only temporary—

that à la the silver lizards
Robert Frost purported to have
seen cascading down the
mountainside in slush-time,
    this time the furry

entity you knew, if not quite
yet dissolved into a dew, will
have surrendered to the texture
of that habitat, the slither
    of its understory.

Yet when you call the name you've
given him, that like a skipped
stone skims the surface of what-
ever's out there, something,
    primed to be ready for a

game of shake-and-bake, a fondling
session, with the inevitable risk
of being laughed at—is it habit,
is it altogether voluntary?—
    brings him in a hurry.

GOOSEBERRY FOOL

The gooseberry's no doubt an oddity,
an outlaw or pariah even—thorny
and tart as any
kindergarten martinet, it can harbor
like a fernseed, on its leaves' under-
side, bad news for pine trees,
whereas the spruce
resists the blister rust
it's host to. That veiny Chinese
lantern, its stolid jelly
of a fruit, not only has
no aroma but is twice as tedious
as the wild strawberry's sunburst
stem-end appendage: each one must
be between-nail-snipped at both extremities.

Altogether, gooseberry virtues
take some getting
used to, much as does trepang,
tripe à la mode de Caen,
or having turned thirteen.
The acerbity of all things green
and adolescent lingers in
it—the arrogant, shrinking,
prickling-in-every-direction thorn-
iness that loves no company except its,
or anyhow that's what it gets:
bristling up through gooseberry ghetto sprawl
are braced thistles' silvery, militantly symmetrical
defense machineries. Likewise inseparably en-
tangled in the disarray of an
uncultivated childhood, where gooseberry bushes (since
rooted out) once flourished, is
the squandered volupté of lemon-
yellow-petaled roses' luscious flimflam—
an inkling of the mingling into one experience
of suave and sharp, whose supremely im-

probable and far-fetched culinary
embodiment is a gooseberry fool.

Tomorrow, having stumbled into
this trove of chief ingredients
(the other being very thickest cream)
I'll demonstrate it for you. Ever since,
four summers ago, I brought you,
a gleeful Ariel, the trophy
of a small sour handful,
I've wondered what not quite articulated thing
could render magical
the green globe of an unripe berry.
I think now it was simply
the great globe itself's too much to carry.

THE SPRUCE HAS NO TAPROOT

Cats, as a rule, don't take to travel
any better than the lobed, immobile
lichen whose tenure in the rock's
bleak niches, though it lacks
roots, is all but fanatical.

Likewise the cinquefoil: though nebulous
of flower head and petal
as a yard of dotted Swiss,
it keeps, under the froufrou, a profile
low as any fugitive's. The strawberry's

red skeins crisscross the gravel
with such rigor you might suppose
it knew the habitat to be untenable
unless tied down. So do the rootstocks
of the rose its cousin, whose colonies

along the coast rise as they widen
into a mimic mountain.
Depth isn't everything: the spruce
has no taproot, but to hold on
spreads its underpinnings thin—

a gathering in one continuous,
meshing intimacy, the interlace
of unrelated fibers
joining hands like last survivors
who, though not even neighbors

hitherto, know in their predicament
security at best is shallow.
Whoever fancies an uprooted fragment
of the coast of Maine might settle into
a New York apartment—foolish,

unnatural whim!—discovers what
must have possessed the cat
when, rather than go through
one more uprooting, she hid out,
a fugitive fanatic who

instead preferred to starve and stiffen.
Found too late, according to her wish
what's left of her is now in-
extricable from the ground. Every
day for weeks, half a can of Figaro

flavored with liver or tunafish
waited out there for her. Every night
for weeks, some mobile opportunist
slipped in from the forest
to banquet from her dish.

WHAT THE LIGHT WAS LIKE

*For Louise Dickinson Rich and
the family of Ernest Woodward*

Every year in June—up here, that's the month for lilacs—
        almost his whole front yard,
with lobster traps stacked out in back, atop the rise
        that overlooks the inlet
would be a Himalayan range of peaks of bloom,
        white or mauve-violet,

gusting a turbulence of perfume, and every year the same
        iridescent hummingbird,
or its descendant, would be at work among the mourning cloaks
        and swallowtails, its motor loud,
its burning gorget darkening at moments as though charred.
        He kept an eye out

for it, we learned one evening, as for everything that flapped
        or hopped or hovered
crepuscular under the firs: he'd heard the legendary
        trilling of the woodcock,
and watched the eiders, once rare along these coasts,
        making their comeback

so that now they're everywhere, in tribes, in families
        of aunts and cousins,
a knit-and-purl of irresistibly downy young behind them, riding
        every cove and inlet;
and yes, in answer to the question summer people always ask,
        he'd seen the puffins

that breed out on 'Tit Manan, in summer improbably clown-faced
        behind the striped scarlet
of Commedia dell' Arte masks we'll never see except in
        Roger Tory Peterson's
field guide, or childish wishful thinking. There was much
        else I meant to ask about

another summer. But in June, when we came limping up here
        again, looking forward
to easing up from a mean, hard, unaccommodating winter,
        we heard how he'd gone out
at dawn, one morning in October, unmoored the dinghy
        and rowed to his boat

as usual, the harbor already chugging with half a dozen
        neighbors' revved-up craft,
wet decks stacked abaft with traps, the bait and kegs stowed
        forward, a lifting weft
of fog spooled off in pearl-pink fleeces overhead with the first
        daylight, and steered,

as usual, past first the inner and then the outer bar, where in
        whatever kind of weather,
the red reef-bell yells, in that interminable treble, *Trouble,*
        out past where the Groaner
lolls, its tempo and forte changing with the chop, played on
        by every wind shift,

straight into the sunrise, a surge of burning turning the
        whole ocean iridescent
fool's-gold over molten emerald, into the core of that
        day-after-day amazement—
a clue, one must suppose, to why lobstermen are often
        naturally gracious:

maybe, out there beside the wheel, the Baptist spire
        shrunk to a compass-
point, the town an interrupted circlet, feeble as an apron-
        string, for all the labor
it took to put it there, it's finding, out in that ungirdled
        wallowing and glitter,

finally, that what you love most is the same as what you're
        most afraid of—God,
in a word; whereas it seems they think they've got it licked
        (or used to), back there
in the Restricted Area for instance, where that huge hush-
        hush thing they say is radar

sits sprawling on the heath like Stonehenge, belittling every
        other man-made thing
in view, even the gargantuan pods of the new boat hulls you
        now and then see lying,
stark naked, crimson on the inside as a just-skinned carcass,
        in Young's boatyard,

even the gray Grange Hall, wood-heated by a yardarm of stovepipe
        across the ceiling.
Out there, from that wallowing perspective, all comparisons
        amount to nothing,
though once you've hauled your last trap, things tend to wander
        into shorter focus

as, around noon, you head back in: first 'Tit Manan lighthouse,
        a ghostly gimlet
on its ledge by day, but on clear nights expanding to a
        shout, to starboard,
the sunstruck rock pile of Cranberry Point to port; then
        you see the hamlet

rainbowed, above the blurring of the spray shield, by the
        hurrying herring gulls'
insatiable fandango of excitement—the spire first, then
        the crimson boat hulls,
the struts of the ill-natured gadget on the heath behind them
        as the face of things expands,

the hide-and-seek behind the velvet-shouldered, sparse
        tree-spined profiles,
as first the outer, then the inner bar appears, then the scree-
        beach under Crowley Island's
crowding firs and spruces, and you detect among the chimneys
        and the TV aerials,

yours. But by midafternoon of that October day,
        when all his neighbors'
boats had chugged back through the inlet, his
        was still out; at evening,
with half the town out looking, and a hard frost
        settling in among the alders,

there'd been no sign of him. The next day, and the next,
        the search went on,
and widened, joined by planes and helicopters from as
        far away as Boston.
When, on the third day, his craft was sighted
        finally, it had drifted,

with its engine running, till the last gulp of fuel
        spluttered and ran out,
beyond the town's own speckled noose of buoys, past
        the furred crest of Schoodic,
vivid in a skirt of aspens, the boglands cranberry-
        crimson at its foot,

past the bald brow the sunrise always strikes first, of
        the hulk of Cadillac,
riding the current effortlessly as eiders tied to water
        by the summer molt,
for fifty miles southwestward to where, off Matinicus,
        out past the rock

that, like 'Tit Manan, is a restricted area, off limits for
　　　　all purposes but puffins',
they spotted him, slumped against the kegs. I find it
　　　　tempting to imagine what,
when the blood roared, overflowing its cerebral sluiceway,
　　　　and the iridescence

of his last perception, charring, gave way to unreversed,
　　　　irrevocable dark,
the light out there was like, that's always shifting—from
　　　　a nimbus gone berserk
to a single gorget, a cathedral train of blinking, or
　　　　the fogbound shroud

that can turn anywhere into a nowhere. But it's useless.
　　　　Among the mourning-cloak-
hovered-over lilac peaks, their whites and purples,
　　　　when we pass his yard,
poignant to excess with fragrance, this year we haven't
　　　　seen the hummingbird.

BLACK BUTTERCUPS

In March, the farmer's month
for packing up and moving on, the rutted
mud potholed with glare, the verb *to move*
connoted nothing natural, such as the shifting
of the course of streams or of the sun's
position, sap moving up, or even
couples dancing. What the stripped root, exhumed
above the mudhole's brittle skin, discerned
was exile.
      Exile to raw clapboard,
a privy out in back, a smokehouse
built by the pioneers, no shade trees
but a huddle of red cedars, exposure
on the highest elevation in the township,
a gangling windmill harped on by each
indisposition of the weather,
the mildewed gurgle of a cistern
humped underneath it like a burial.
         Menace
inhabited that water when the pioneers,
ending their trek from North Carolina, farther
than Ur of the Chaldees had been from Canaan,
settled here and tried to root themselves:
four of the family struck down on this farm
as its first growing season ended. Menace
still waited, literally around the corner,
in the graveyard of a country church,
its back against the timber
just where the terrain began to drop (the creek
down there had for a while powered a sawmill,
but now ran free, unencumbered, useless)—
that not-to-be-avoided plot whose honed stones'
fixed stare, fanned in the night
by passing headlights, struck back
the rueful semaphore:
There is no safety.

                                    I was ten years old.
Not three miles by the road that ran
among the farms (still less if
you could have flown, or, just as unthinkable,
struck out across country, unimpeded
by barbed wire or the mire of feedlots)
the legendary habitat of safety
lay contained: the memory
of the seedleaf in the bean, the blind
hand along the bannister, the virgin sheath
of having lived nowhere but here. Back there
in the dining room, last summer's
nine-year-old sat crying on the window seat
that looked into the garden, rain
coursing the pane in streams, the crying
on the other side and it one element—and sits
there still, still crying, knowing
for the first time forever what it was
to be heartbroken.
                                    The look of exile
foreseen, however massive or inconsequential,
hurts the same; it's the remembered
particulars that differ. How is one to measure
the loss of two blue spruces, a waterfall
of bridal wreath below the porch, the bluebells
and Dutchman's-breeches my grandmother
had brought in from the timber
to bloom in the same plot with peonies
and lilies of the valley? Or, out past
the pasture where the bull, perennially
resentful, stood for the menace of authority
(no leering, no snickering in class),
an orchard—or a grove of willows
at the far edge of the wet meadow
marking the verge, the western barrier
of everything experience had verified? We never
thought of going there except in February,

when the sap first started working up
the pussywillow wands, the catkins
pink underneath a down of eldritch silver
like the new pigs whose birthing coincided,
shedding their crisp cupolas' detritus
on the debris of foundering snowbanks
brittle as the skin of standing ponds
we trod on in the meadow, a gauche travesty
of calamity like so many entertainments—
the nuptial porcelain, the heirloom crystal
vandalized by wanton overshoes, bundled-up
boredom lolling, while the blue world reeled
up past the pussywillow undersides of clouds
latticed by swigging catkins soon to haze
with pollen-bloat, a glut
run riot while the broken pond
unsealed, turned to mud
and, pullulating, came up buttercups
lucent with a mindlessness as total
as the romp that ends up wet-mittened,
chap-cheeked, fretful beside the kitchen stove,
later to roughhouse or whine its way
upstairs to bed.
                          Night froze it up again
for the ten thousandth time, closing the seals
above the breeding ground of frogs, the Acheron
of dreadful disappointed Eros
stirring up hell—the tics,
the shame, the pathological ambition,
anxiety so thick sometimes that nothing
breeds there except more anxiety,
hampering yet another generation, all
the sodden anniversaries of dread:
black buttercups that never see daylight
or with lucent chalices drink of the sun.
Did we then hear them moving
wounded from room to room? Or in what shape

was it we first perceived it—the unstanched
hereditary thing, working its way
along the hollows of the marrow,
the worry taking root within like ragweed,
the noxious pollen flowering into
nothing but sick headaches
passed down like an heirloom? When,
under the same roof the memory of
a legendary comfort had endowed
with what in retrospect would seem
like safety, did the rumor
of unhappiness arrive? I remember waking,
a February morning leprous with frost
above the dregs of a halfhearted snowfall,
to find the gray world of adulthood
everywhere, as though there never
had been any other, in that same house
I could not bear to leave, where even now
the child who wept to leave still sits
weeping at the thought of exile.

WITNESS

An ordinary evening in Wisconsin
seen from a Greyhound bus—mute aisles
of merchandise the sole inhabitants
of the half-darkened Five and Ten,

the tables of the single lit café awash
with unarticulated pathos, the surface membrane
of the inadvertently transparent instant
when no one is looking: outside town

the barns, their red gone dark with sundown,
withhold the shudder of a warped terrain—
the castle rocks above, tree-clogged ravines
already submarine with nightfall, flocks

(like dark sheep) of toehold junipers,
the lucent arms of birches : purity
without a mirror, other than a mind bound
elsewhere, to tell it how it looks.

URN-BURIAL AND
THE BUTTERFLY MIGRATION

Rest for the body's residue:
boxed ashes, earth pocket
under its lifted flap of turf
roofed by a black circumference
of Norway spruce, an old settler
now among old settlers, in their
numb stones' cooled silicates
the scar of memory benighted
alone articulate.

O friable repose of the organic!
Bark-creviced at the trunk's
foot, ladybirds' enameled herds
gather for the winter, red pearls
of an unsaid rosary to waking.
From the fenced beanfield,
crickets' brisk scrannel
plucks the worn reed of
individual survival.

Mulleins hunker to a hirsute
rosette about the taproot; from
frayed thistleheads, a liftoff
of aerial barbs begins; milkweed
spills on the wind its prodigal,
packed silks—slattern gondolas
whose wrecked stalks once
gave mooring to the sleep of
things terrestrial:

an urn of breathing jade, its
gilt-embossed exterior the
intact foreboding of a future
intricately contained, jet-
veined, spangle-margined,
birth-wet russet of the air-
traveling monarch emerging

from a torpid chrysalis. Oh,
we know nothing

of the universe we move through!
My dead brother, when we were
kids, fed milkweed caterpillars
in Mason jars, kept bees, ogled
the cosmos through a backyard
telescope. But then the rigor
of becoming throttled our pure
ignorance to mere haste
toward something else.

We scattered. Like the dandelion,
that quintessential successful
immigrant, its offspring gone
to fluff, dug-in hard-scrabble
nurtured a generation of
the mobile, nomads enamored
of cloverleafs, of hangars, of
that unrest whose home—*our*
home—is motion.

Here in the winds' terrain, the
glacier-abraded whetstone of their
keening knives, anvil of thunder,
its sabbaths one treacherous
long sob of apprehension, who
will rein in, harpoon or anchor
rest for the mind? Were the dead
to speak, were one day
these friable

residues to rise, would we hear
even that airborne murmur? Listen
as the monarchs' late-emerging
tribes ascend; you will hear

nothing. In wafted twos and threes
you may see them through the window
of a southbound Greyhound
bus, adrift across the
Minnesota border;

or in flickering clots, in dozens
above the parked cars of the
shopping malls of Kansas—this
miracle that will not live to
taste the scarce nectar, the
ample horror of another summer:
airborne marathon, elegiac
signature of nations who
have no language,

their landless caravans augment
among the blistered citadels
of Oklahoma; windborne along
the Dallas–Fort Worth airport's
utopian thoroughfares, their
hovering millenniums become
a mimic force of occupation,
a shadeless Vallombrosa,
forceless, autonomous.

O drifting apotheosis of dust
exhumed, who will unseal
the crypt locked up within
the shimmer of the chromosomes,
or harvest, from the alluvial
death-dance of these wrecked
galaxies, this risen residue
of milkweed leaf and honey,
rest for the body?

HIGH CULTURE

The geranium and the begonia
bloom with such offhand redundance
we scarcely notice. But the
amaryllis is a study in

disruption: everything routine
gives way to the unsheathing
of its climbing telescope—
a supernova of twin crimson

tunnels, porches of infinity
where last week there was nothing.
Months of clandestine preparation
now implode in pollen

that will never brush a bee,
fueling the double-barreled velvet
stairwell of its sterile pistils
with a tapered incandescence

that's already short of breath
and going blind before a
week is out. Such show
of breeding, such an excess

of cultivation, all but asks us
to stop breathing too until
it's over. I remember
how, the night the somewhat

famous violinist came to supper,
the whisper of the gown she
put on just before the concert
filled the parlor of the farmhouse

with things it had no room for—
the slave marts of the East,
the modes of Paris, the gazing
ramparts of the stratosphere.

VOYAGES:
A HOMAGE TO JOHN KEATS

For Helen Vendler

Cowslip and shad-blow, flaked like tethered foam
Around bared teeth of stallions, bloomed that spring
When I first read the lines, rife as the loam
Of prairies, yet like breakers cliffward leaping!
      . . . My hand
         in yours,
         Walt Whitman . . .

                        HART CRANE, *The Bridge*

Chaff, straw, splinters of wood, weeds, and the sea-gluten,
Scum, scales from shining rocks, leaves of salt-lettuce, left by the tide,
Miles walking, the sound of breaking waves the other side of me,
Paumanok there and then I thought the old thought of likenesses,
These you presented to me you fish-shaped island . . .

                        WALT WHITMAN, "Sea-Drift"

Perhaps my whisper was already born before my lips,
the leaves whirled round in treelessness
and those to whom we dedicate our life's experience
before experience acquired their traits.

                        OSIP MANDELSTAM
                        (Moscow, January 1934)

. . . a haggling of wind and weather, by these lights
Like a blaze of summer straw, in winter's nick.

                        WALLACE STEVENS,
                        "The Auroras of Autumn"

MARGATE

Reading his own lines over, he'd been
(he wrote) in the diminished state of one
"that gathers Samphire dreadful trade."
Disabled Gloucester, so newly eyeless
all his scathed perceptions bled together,
and Odysseus, dredged up shipwrecked
through fathoms of Homeric sightlessness—

"the sea had soaked his heart through"—
were the guides his terror clutched at.
Now all of twenty-one, he'd written nothing
of moment but one bookish sonnet: "Much have
I traveled . . ." Only he hadn't, other
than as unrequited amateur. How clannish
the whole hand-to-hand, cliffhanging trade,

the gradual letdown, the hempen slither,
precarious basketloads of sea drift
gathered at Margate or at Barnegat:
along Paumanok's liquid rim, the dirges,
nostalgia for the foam: *the bottom of*
the sea is cruel. The chaff, the scum
of the impalpable confined in stanzas,

a shut-in's hunger for the bodiless
enkindlings of the aurora—all that
traffic in the perilous. That summer,
orphaned of sublimity, he'd settled for
the way an oatfield's stalks and blades
checquered his writing tablet with their
quivering. But after, back in Hampstead,

the samphire-gatherer's mimic god-deliverer
still bled metonymy: an ordinary field of
barley turned to alien corn's inland sea-
surfaces, and onto every prairie rolling,
sans the samphire trade's frail craft, un-
  basketed, undid the casement of the homesick,
  stared once more, and called an image home.

TEIGNMOUTH

Even in mild Devon, that spring, the lung-
destroying English climate was one long
dank rampage: high winds, trees falling
onto the roads, stagecoaches overturning,

day upon day of drumming, streaming rain
swollen to weeks, the sun a half-believed-in
pagan god above the azure of the Mediterranean.
At night he'd lie in bed (he wrote) and listen

to it with a sense of being drowned and rotted
like a grain of wheat. He very nearly hated
Tom because he coughed so; then his raw mood
froze as he saw his brother cough up blood.

His writing plodded. By now *Endymion* bored him.
His letters joked of waterspouts and rattraps. Rhyme,
that light-fingered habit, ran down and went grim:
beyond an untumultuous fringe of foam,

he'd seen, once the weather eased, into a maw
of rot, a predatory core of dying. Melodrama
mildewed the sources of romance: the basil grew
rank from her dead lover's skull for Isabella.

What might still flower out of that initiation
to the sodden underside of things—those Eleusinian
passageways that seem (he wrote) only to darken
as the doors of new and vaster chambers open—

he could no more than guess at. On May Day
he looked from the window of a single stanza
leaning toward Theocritus and the blue Bay
of Baiae (read Naples). Not yet twenty-three,

he'd presently begin to resurrect, to all but
deify the issue of his own wretched climate—
primroses, cress and water-mint, great wet-
globed peonies, the grape against the palate:

an *annus mirabilis* of odes before the season
of the oozing of the ciderpress, the harvest done,
wheatfields blood-spattered once with poppies gone
to stubble now, the swallows fretting to begin

their windborne flight toward a Mediterranean
that turned to marble as the mists closed in
on the imagination's yet untrodden region—
the coal-damps, the foul winter dark of London.

THE ELGIN MARBLES

For Frederick Turner

Openings. Winandermere and Derwentwater.
The Elgin Marbles. That last evening
at the Crown in Liverpool, with George
and his new wife, imagination failed

    —and still fails: what can John Keats
    have had to do with a hacked clearing
    in the Kentucky underbrush? How could
    Mnemosyne herself, the mother of the Muse,
    have coped with that uncultivated tangle,
    catbrier and poison ivy, chiggers,
    tent caterpillars, cottonmouths,
    the awful gurglings and chirrings
    of the dark?

                    Turning his back
against the hemp and tar, the
creaking tedium of actual departure,
the angry fogs, the lidless
ferocity of the Atlantic—epic
distances fouled by necessity—
he left them sleeping, George
and his Georgiana, so much wrapped up
in being newly wed they scarcely knew
they had no home now but each other,
he took up his pack (a change of
clothes, pens, paper, the *Divine
Comedy* in translation—he knew no
Italian yet, or Greek) and headed north,
on foot, with his friend Brown. Rain
held them up a day, but on
the twenty-sixth of June (a letter
to his brother Tom records) they came
in sight of Winandermere. He stared,
then slowly swore, "This—
must—beat—Italy."

                              Imaginary
          Italy, the never-never
          vista, framed, of Stresa
          on Lago Maggiore, to badger
          an imagination starved for charm,
          for openings, living on cornpone,
          coonskin, literary hand-me-downs,
          and hating everything in sight.

                              Hyperbole:
          a vista, as he put it, to make one forget
          what tended to cut off, refining what he called
          the Sensual Vision into—he fumbled for
          an image—a sort of North Star, open-
          lidded, steadfast. Winandermere:
          the Italy he'd never seen, though in
          imagination he already lived there:
          his mind's America. Bright star.
          Made one forget the creak, the tar,
          the lunging hulk, homesick, sea-
          sick, of the Atlantic.

                              Or almost did.
          Next day, at Helvellyn (mist about its foot
          so thick he never saw it, the Nag's Head
          flea-infested) he invoked,
          in an acrostic on Georgiana's name, Odysseus
          stormed at sea, and after
          Derwentwater and Lodore made weak amends
          with fact by conjuring a doggerel prospect
          "where furrows are new to the plow."
          After Skiddaw—a ten-mile hike,
          made fasting, having gotten up
          at four—they took a coach
          for Scotland.

The tomb of Burns.
Pinched lives. Bad food. A fog
of whisky. The cold, pale, short-
lived, primeval summer. He was tired now,
homesick for another kind of grandeur:
Lord Elgin's windlass-lowered metopes ("A sun—
a shadow of a magnitude," he'd written
of the space they opened). Scotland
seemed—the epithet broke from him—
anti-Grecian. Admitting prejudice,
he repented, tried whisky-toddy,
wrote a ballad, saw the poverty, grew somber
as he thought of Burns, observing his imagination
had been southern too; caught a cold
he couldn't shake, grew peevish,
cut short his tour. In Hampstead,
Tom had been coughing blood again.

                              Another
summer gone, Tom worse, his own sore throat
recurring, *Endymion* stillborn, picked over
by the vultures. Well,
they were partly right; the rest he wouldn't
think about. Now, primed on *Lear,*
Milton, Gibbon, Wordsworth, he'd set himself
to re-imagining an epic grandeur, such as
(if it arrived at all) came battered
and diminished, fallen like Lucifer,
or else dismantled, fragmentary, lowered and
transported, piece by piece, like the heroic
torsos, the draperied recumbent hulks Lord Elgin
took down from the Parthenon.

                              —Behold,
   in the back settlements, the rise
   of Doric porticoes. Courthouse
   spittoons. The glimmer of a classic

colonnade through live oaks. Slave
cabins. Mud. New Athenses, Corinths,
Spartas among the Ossabaws and
Tuscaloosas, the one no less
homesick than the other for
what never was, most likely,
but in some founder's warped
and sweating mind.

                              Ruin alone,
in a bad time, had seemed to him
grand enough. But then, out of the
still unimagined West, that welter
of a monument to hardship, stirrings
of another sort: Georgiana
was to have a child.

                           Precarious
domestic comfort, a firelit
ring of faces' bright cave
in the Kentucky wilderness: the wonder
of it! Not quite two years
since, in lodgings he and George and Tom,
three orphaned, homeless brothers
had moved into, he'd invoked
just such an image: small, busy flames
playing through fresh-laid
coals, a refuge hollowed from
the gloom of London in November. Now,
out of that solitude, a child,
another Keats, to be the bard of what
John Keats himself could never quite
imagine: he turned the fantasy
into a lullaby, went back
to reconstructing such an inlet
to severe magnificence
as a god might enter. "I think

I shall be among the English
poets after my death." There,
he'd said it.

                    The evening of
October twenty-fourth (a date that,
once again, would go on record),
walking from Bedford Row to Lamb's
Conduit Street, he met the enigmatic
Mrs. Isabella Jones, and walked her home.
Her sitting room a trove of bronze,
books, pictures, music (an Aeolian
harp, a linnet): rich and somber—moonlight
through diamond panes, a Turkish carpet—
was the way he'd re-imagine it. A
prior contretemps seemed to require
some move. Tactfully declining to
be kissed, however, she released him
to a state of mind that was—
he discovered, walking home
astonished—infinitely
better:
                    He was free.
He could imagine anything at all,
needed no home, would never marry—not
though the carpet there were silk,
the curtain made of morning cloud, with windows
that opened on Winandermere. The roaring
of the wind, he wrote (hyperbole again, but
never mind) would be his wife, the stars
seen through the windows would be his children.
A perfect solitude. A thousand worlds thrown open.
He was as happy as a man could be—or would be,
he conscientiously amended, if Tom were better.

Bright star. Winandermere. A week
from now, he would be twenty-three.

CHICHESTER

There would have been the obligatory tour
of the cathedral. Stone under boot heels,
the great, numbed ribcage chilled-to-the-bone
cold. The aisles of sculptured effigies stone
dead. Tom dead at the beginning of December.
It was January now. Buried at St. Stephen's
Coleman Street. The bare spire, the leafless
trees. The church bells' interminable reminder.
One Sunday evening, hearing them, he'd dashed
off—with Tom there in the room, timing him—
a sonnet "In Disgust of Vulgar Superstition."
Here, the recurrent chatter of those great
metal tongues would have brought it back,
setting his memory on edge again. *Poor Tom*.
The scene out on the heath forever lurking
in his mind. Back in October he'd underlined
the words: Poor Tom. Poor Tom's a-cold.

His friends meant well, had kept him occupied.
Visits. A play. Dragged him down to Sussex
for a prizefight. Mrs. Isabella Jones, with
new notions for him to write about. Miss
Brawne: beautiful, elegant, graceful, silly,
fashionable and strange. He'd set down the
words with care. It was important to keep
things accurate. A minx—he'd called her
that, and also ignorant, monstrous in her
behavior, flying out in all directions, calling
people such names. Hair nicely arranged.
Loved clothes. Eighteen years old. Down here,
best not to think very much about her. Brown
playing the fool, putting on an old lady's
bonnet. At night, old dowager card parties.
As always, the anxiety about getting down
to work. No progress with the epic since Tom
died. Isabella Jones urging him to try another

romance. Why not, she'd said, the legend
of St. Agnes' Eve? A girl going to bed . . .

He must have whistled at the notion that struck
him now. And then blushed. Or vice versa. A
girl going to bed on St. Agnes' Eve—that very
night, or near it—without supper, so as to
dream of the man she was to marry. Imagine
her. Imagine . . . He blushed now at the
audacity. But the thing had taken hold:
St. Agnes' Eve. A girl going to bed . . .
On the twenty-third of January, they walked
thirteen miles, to a little town called (of
all things) Bedhampton. The house they stayed
in there still stands. Out of the frozen
countryside they'd passed through, once his
numb hands had thawed, he had what he needed
to begin: the owl, the limping hare, the
woolly huddle inside the sheepfold. Even
the owl a-cold. *Poor Tom.* The cold stone
underfoot, the sculptured effigies. How
they must ache. His own numb fingers. How
the Beadsman's hands must ache. Paid to hold
a rosary for the souls of others richer and
more vicious. The stones he knelt on cold.
The girl's bedchamber cold, the bed itself
too, until the girl—blushing, he saw her
kneel—had warmed it. He saw it all.

He saw it: saw the candle in the icy draft
gone out, the little smoke, the moonlight,
the diamond panes, the stained-glass colors
on her as she knelt to say her silly prayers.
Saw her, smelled her, felt the warmth of the
unfastened necklace, the brooch, the earrings,
heard the rustle as the dress slid down;
backed off, became the voyeur of a mermaid.
Discovered, while she slept, that the sheets

gave off a sachet of lavender. Admired but
did not taste the banquet his senses had
invented, and whose true name was Samarkand.
He was in fact too excited to eat. What is
a poet to do when he stumbles onto such
excitement? He was not sure. He was also
somewhat embarrassed. Later he'd declare,
hotly, that he wrote for men, not ladies
(who are the ones who dream such things),
that he'd despise any man who was such a
eunuch as not to avail himself . . . It was
the flaw, as he must have known. He'd
imagined it all. He'd imagined it all.

For ten days that lush, decorated stanza,
with its shut casements and dying fall,
had been the room he lived in. He'd
imagined it all; his senses had seduced
an entire posterity into imagining what
had never happened. His own virgin vision,
of a solitude that needed no wife, had been
seduced by that imaginary place, that stanza,
where nothing at all had happened. The minx
who was eighteen, beautiful, silly, strange
and fond of clothes, and who had never lived
there, was real. The cold outside was real.
Dying was real, and the twitch of the old
woman's palsy. The effigies were real,
and the stones in the churchyard at St.
Stephen's Coleman Street. *Poor Tom.*

HE DREAMS OF BEING WARM

The April he'd invoked from the despond
of February (when his sore throat
came back)—its hillsides starred
by an upended firmament of daisies—
found him straining at particles of
light in a great darkness, bright-eyed
underfoot with scurryings of purpose:
the alert stoat, the quivering fieldmouse,
the lowlife fracases he'd seen erupting
in the streets of London—instinct in
the bud, the blood stirred in a poor
forked creature battered by the same
mischances, subject to the same
       inclement weather.

On the eleventh day of April he
shook the hand of Coleridge, and
felt warmed. But the low mood that
had hampered him continued. *Hyperion*,
he knew now after a final try—*Apollo*
shrieked—and lo! from all his limbs
celestial . . . would not be completed.
How could he not think with irony of
that *celestial?* The foreign sun-god,
aloof familiar of the Muse, once-blazing
luminary now a mere pinprick, remote
among the other stars—himself left
shivering, abandoned to the merciless
catarrhs of London. Infernal visions
drew him: not now that scathing splendor,
the lyre, the paean, the white glare
of sunstruck marble, but the wailing
shades, the cranes' cry, the starlings
interminably circling: imagined torments
       of felicity remembered.

April in hell, a courteous reception
to the circle of the lustful: the dream
he'd had came back as pure enjoyment.
Welcomed by Francesca, late of Rimini,
into the storm of starlings, joined
to another solely by a kiss, for what
had seemed an aeon's celestial levitation,
he had been happy: in the midst of all
that cold and darkness, *he was warm.*
April in hell: a firmament upended
to a stirred greensward of treetops
that, tiptoe, he felt expanding into
secret zodiacs of blossom. And then
        woke. And shivered.

Outside, it was raining. He stayed in
all day, attempting in a sonnet—"Pale
were the lips I kissed"—to summon
back the dream. Damp, half-charred
firewood brought in from the rain,
it wouldn't kindle—until, on the
twenty-first of April, in an aubade
set to the starved meter of a ballad,
he harpooned the levitating kiss, and
quartered it. (Why *four* kisses?—Because,
he quipped, the Muse needs reining in.
Suppose I had said seven?) So adieu,
Francesca, late of Rimini. Farewell,
imaginary region of the headlong; even
your lusts cannot (it seems) delude so well
as the received morality would have it.
Dream of being warm, farewell.
Exposure on a cold hillside,
        good morning.

April long gone, the sedges dead
and withered: wake, poor fool, to agues
of the morning after—to having been,
from your brief *saison en enfer,*
locked out, the ecstasy aborted,
masked Melancholy's sable domino
torn off, the Muse herself disclosed,
in the strict morning light, as an
unforthcoming warden: no comfort,
only carnage underfoot, a cutthroat
cunning prowling the streets of
London—and waking, one among
the many, from dim dreams, harbored
numberless as vermin, of being warm,
to freezing on this houseless,
      flowerless hillside.

THE ISLE OF WIGHT

Toward the end of April, for an idyllic
   week, the rain stopped, and on the third
of May he wrote, "O there is nothing like
   fine weather, health, Books, a contented
Mind . . ." The ballad's nightmare hillside
   turned, on a burst of bloom, into a picnic:
Psyche, poor butterfly-winged, put-upon immortal,
   last met with in the cold of that starved bedrock,
translated, bless her, to shameless daylit *al*
   fresco, the flowery upheaval of the marriage bed.

Reclaimed thus for Eros, what had he to offer?
   Rash promises, no more. He'd build (he wrote)
a sanctuary purely of the mind, in some far-
   off, untrodden region, with a window in it
left open every night, not now to frame
   the stars (if any) but to admit a visitor
prohibited the homelier usages of daylight.
   A sanctuary of the mind, no more. That summer,
cooped with a Bacchic leopard on the Isle of Wight,
   he'd wish he'd never offered it house room.

"Ask yourself my love whether you are not
   very cruel to have so destroyed my freedom,"
he wrote—hyperbole such as he'd often laughed at.
   But now he'd let this hot sprite in, the gloom
of sundown brought home, night after night,
   to that room he said was like a coffin,
no ornate access such as had beguiled him—
   no casement triple-arched as on the night,
long gone, those lovers fled into the storm:
   the framework of escape had shut him in.

His sore throat had come back in June; he saw
   still no prospect of a settled income,
could not live with her but could not now sue
   love for a retraction. Shut up with phantom

rivals in that little room at Shanklin,
     where was the old, wild pleasure of a window
opening on a view of water?—Sealed off like a poem
     he might have written once but couldn't now—
its magic casements closed against the spume
     and spindrift of a serpentine illusion.

Illusion, snared in a brisk running couplet,
     was his new preoccupation—the dazed lamé
of its phosphorescent moons, its shivering scarlet
     and skewered emeralds a weird trophy
hung among the totems of his own ambivalence:
     he almost yearned, he'd written at the start,
for metempsychosis as an insect—for just three
     butterfly-winged summer days' intensity. *Delight,*
he'd called it: poor worn-out word. Poor Psyche,
     poor feeble suffix of doubtful provenance!

WINCHESTER:
THE AUTUMN EQUINOX

Salubrious air, free of the low fogs that were
(he wrote) like steam from cabbage water;
past scrubbed stoops and ram's-head-knockered
doors, a daily walk through the cathedral yard
down to the river: how beautiful
the season was—ay, better than
the chilly green of spring, the warmed hue
of grainfields' harsh stubs turned pictorial
with equinoctial bloom, the tincture of
the actual, the mellow aftermath of fever:
purgatorial winnowings, the harvest over.

Seamless equipoise of crossing: Nox,
primordial half-shape above the treadle,
the loomed fabric of the sun-god's ardor
foreshortened, with a roar as if of earthly
fire, all twilit Europe at his back,
toward the threshold of the west: *in me
thou seest such twilight, in me thou seest
the glowing of such fire as after sunset*
floods the west's unentered spaces. Black gates
shut against the sunrise; north and south, a mist
of nothing: the opening was to the west.

The opening of the West: what Miltonic
rocketry of epithet, what paradigm
of splendor in decline, could travel,
and survive, the monstrous region (as he'd
later depict it) of dull rivers poured
from sordid urns, rank tracts unowned
by any weed-haired god he'd ever heard of,
that had fleeced his brother George? "Be careful,"
he wrote, "of those Americans"—meaning
mainly a certain Audubon, of Henderson,
Kentucky. "I can not help thinking Mr. Audubon

has deceived you. I shall not like the sight
of him . . . You will perceive," he'd also
written, "it is quite out of my interest to
come to America. What could I do there? How
could I employ myself ?" John James Audubon,
whether swindler or merely incorrigibly careless,
might carve a kind of wonder, a fierce, frightful
elegance, out of the houseless openings,
the catbrier-hammock deadfalls of that
unfenced paradise. But what could Milton,
from whom he'd set himself to learn, have done

to clear a path either for grandeur or
for simple ruth to enter? Look homeward—
where? What images, what language, fossil
child of all the dislocations of antiquity,
could clear that threshold? *Like the mild moon
who comforts those she sees not, who knows not
what eyes are upward cast*, Moneta, Shade
of Memory, Admonisher, when called upon—
whereon (he wrote) *there grew a power within me
of enormous ken*—showed only splendor fallen.
His peace made with the diminishments of autumn,

he now declared the second epic of the sun-
god's fall abandoned.
                    Hampstead: Fever
and passion. A comedy. A sonnet. In letters,
now and then a cry of protest. The rest
is posthumous.

VOYAGES

On April twenty-seventh, 1932, Hart Crane
walked to the taffrail of the *Orizaba,*
took off his coat, and leaped. At seventeen,
a changeling from among the tire-and-rubber

factories, steel mills, cornfields of the Ohio
flatland that had absent-mindedly produced him,
on an enthralled first voyage he'd looked into
the troughed Caribbean, and called it home.

Back where he'd never been at home, he'd once
watched the early-morning shift pour down South Main—
immigrant Greeks eager to be Americans—
and then tried to imagine Porphyro in Akron

(Greek for "high place"): the casement, the arras,
the fabricated love nest, the actual sleet storm,
the owl, the limping hare, the frozen grass,
Keats's own recurring dream of being warm—

who'd been so often cold he looked with yearning even
into blacksmiths' fires: "How glorious," he wrote
of them, shivering (with Stevens) to see the stars put on
their glittering belts: of what disaster was that

chill, was that salt wind the imminence? The cold-
a-long-time, lifetime snow man did not know.
Beside the Neva, Osip Mandelstam wrote of the cold,
the December fog-blurs of Leningrad. O to throw

open (he wrote) a window on the Adriatic!—a window
for the deprived of audience, for the unfree
to breathe, to breathe even the bad air of Moscow.
Yet on the freezing pane of perpetuity,

that coruscating cold-frame fernery of breath,
harsh flowerbed of the unheated rooms of childhood,
even from the obscurity that sealed it off, his breath,
his warmth, he dared declare, had already settled.

The dream of being warm, its tattered cargo
brought too late to Italy, a mere dire fistful
of blood (*the sea had soaked his heart through*):
the voyage, every voyage at the end is cruel.

In February 1937, from exile to flatland
Voronezh, a kind of twin of Akron, Mandelstam
wrote, in an almost posthumous whisper, of round
blue bays, of sails descried—scenes parted from

as now his voyage to the bottom of a crueler
obscurity began, whose end only the false-haired
seaweed of an inland shipwreck would register.
Untaken voyages, Lethean cold, O all but unendured

arrivals! Keats's starved stare before the actual,
so long imagined Bay of Naples. The mind's extinction.
Nightlong, sleepless beside the Spanish Steps, the prattle
of poured water. Letters no one will ever open.

THE REEDBEDS
OF THE HACKENSACK

Scummed maunderings that nothing loves but reeds,
Phragmites, neighbors of the greeny asphodel
that thrive among the windings of the Hackensack,
collaborating to subvert the altogether ugly
though too down-to-earth to be quite fraudulent:
what's landfill but the backside of civility?

Dreckpot, the Styx and Malebolge of civility,
brushed by the fingering plumes of beds of reeds:
Manhattan's moat of stinks, the rancid asphodel
aspiring from the gradually choking Hackensack,
ring-ditch inferior to the vulgar, the snugly ugly,
knows-no-better, fake but not quite fraudulent:

what's scandal but the candor of the fraudulent?
Miming the burnish of a manicured civility,
the fluent purplings of uncultivated reeds,
ex post cliché survivors like the asphodel,
drink, as they did the Mincius, the Hackensack
in absent-minded benediction on the merely ugly.

Is there a poetry of the incorrigibly ugly,
free of all furbishings that mark it fraudulent?
When toxins of an up-against-the-wall civility
have leached away the last patina of these reeds,
and promised landfill, with its lethal asphodel
of fumes, blooms the slow dying of the Hackensack,

shall I compare thee, Mincius, to the Hackensack?
Now Italy knows how to make its rivers ugly,
must, ergo, all such linkages be fraudulent,
gilding the laureate hearse of a defunct civility?
Smooth-sliding Mincius, crowned with vocal reeds,
coevals of that greeny local weed the asphodel,

that actual, unlettered entity the asphodel,
may I, among the channels of the Hackensack—
those Edens-in-the-works of the irrevocably ugly,
where any mourning would of course be fraudulent—
invoke the scrannel ruth of a forsooth civility,
the rathe, the deathbed generations of these reeds?

REAL ESTATE

Something there is that doesn't
love a Third Avenue tenement,

that wants it gone the way the El
went. Façade a typical example

of red-brick eclectic, its five dozen
windows half now behind blank tin,

scrollwork lintels of strange parentage,
fire escapes' curling-iron birdcage,

are an anomaly among high-rise elevators,
besieged by Urban Relocation (Not A

Governmental Agency). Holdout tenants
confer, gesticulating, by storefronts

adapted only to an anxious present—Le
Boudoir, Le Shampoo, Le Retro (if passé

is chic, is chic passé?). One gelded
pawnshop, until last week, still brooded,

harboring, among tag ends of pathos,
several thirty-year-old umbrellas.

Regularly twice a day, the lingering wraith
within stepped out to shake her dustcloth.

That's done now. She advertised a sale.
Still nothing moved. Finally, a U-Haul

truck carted everything off somewhere.
Hail, real estate! Bravo, entrepreneur!

VACANT LOT WITH
TUMBLEWEED AND PIGEONS

The rooms gone, hallways and stairwells
air, the cornices and fire escapes
where troops of sunning pigeons spun
from common-garden opalescence
the transience of some other thing
more rich and strange, two summers
and a winter solstice since

a dozen dumpsterloads of rubble dis-
embodied what had once seemed settled
here, effaced: the ricepaper
of the first December snowfall
inscribed with a not-yet-uprooted
tumbleweed's whip-limber pyramid,
spare, see-through, symmetrical,

an evergreen in one dimension, each
brushed-in, accidental grass-stroke
beside it letter perfect. Two
summers and a winter solstice
since their perching places went,
pigeons still arrive from somewhere,
and as in a liturgy retrace,

descending yet again the roofless
staircase of outmoded custom, the
soon-to-be-obliterated stations
of nostalgia—as though the air
itself might wince at the stigmata
of the dispossessed, the razed,
the *triste*, the unaccounted-for.

HOMER, A.D. 1982

For Irving Kizner and his class at Hunter College

Much having traveled in the funkier realms of Ac-
ademe, aboard a grungy elevator car,
deus ex machina reversed, to this ninth-floor
classroom, its windows grimy, where the noise of traffic,
πολυφλοίσβοιο-θαλάσσης-like, is chronic,
we've seen since February the stupendous candor
of the *Iliad* pour in, and for an hour and a
quarter at the core the great pulse was dactylic.

We've seen the clash, from those great halls, of light and dark,
the sullen campfires of a brooded-over choler,
Odysseus, rising, sway his peers with storms of logic,
the spurned priest of Apollo shrink along the shore,
and Hector's baby, shadowed by the plumes of war
as we are, pull back from his own father with a shriek.

THE HICKORY GROVE

Flint-skinned, bone-hued
loot from the till of fall—
its draperies all a heap,
the latch left open—
you'll need a hammer
and a brace of nutpicks
to get at the meat of
these obdurate nuggets,

clench-kin to the KEEP OUT
that drives home what matters
is whose woods these are:
a category of autonomy
ignored by squirrels, nor
can the shambling seasons
be neatened and shut into
watertight compartments

such as memory, that burrower,
will undermine with awe,
out there in the bare-
boled, frost-bitten-eared,
enormous silences of winter:
or, alarmingly, the ramrod
shagbarks stirred, up over-
head, into one green-gold

churn of things opening and
unfolding—leaf clusters big
as wheatsheaves cascading
out of casqued sheathings
too extravagant to figure
as a source of income—the
inner burnish of all that
scrap satin such as is un-

amenable to the hard arts
of bronze, of mining and
smelting—or of pouring
an ingot of metaphor so
dazzling, some day some
critic, come round to see
these woods, will post a
sign that says PROPRIETOR.

LOSING TRACK OF LANGUAGE

The train leaps toward Italy, the French Riviera
falls away in the dark, the rails sing dimeter
shifting to trimeter, a gallopade to a galliard.
We sit wedged among strangers; whatever
we once knew (it was never much) of each other
falls away with the landscape. Words
fall away, we trade instead in flirting
and cigarettes; we're all rapport with strangers.
The one with the yellow forelock that keeps falling
and being shaken back again, syncopating
the dimeter-trimeter, gallopade-into-galliard,
is, it seems, Italian—recently a pilgrim
to the Vaucluse, where Petrarca,
to the noise of waterfalls, measured out
his strict stanzas, little rooms
for turmoil to grow lucid in, for
change to put on more durable
leaves of bronze, a scapular of marble.

A splutter of pleasure at hearing the name
is all he needs, and he's off
like a racehorse at the Palio—plunging
unbridled into recited cadenzas, three-beat
lines interleaving a liquid pentameter.
What are words? They fall away into the fleeing
dark of the French Riviera, as once a shower
of bloom, *una pioggia di fior,* descended
into the lap of the Trecento: her hair
all gold and pearl, the grass still warm
as when she sat there, six centuries
gone by; that squandered heartbeat
(the black plague took her, young) now
fossilized as bronze, as carved laurel.
Whatever is left of her is language;
and what is language but breath, leaves,
petals fallen or in the act of falling, pollen
of turmoil that sifts through the fingers?

—*E conosce* (I ask it to keep the torrent
of words from ending, to keep anything
from ending, ever) *anche Sapphò?* Yes,
he knows, he will oblige. The limpid pentameter
gives way to something harsher: diphthongs
condense, take on an edge of bronze. Though
I don't understand a word, what are words? Do these
concern one Timas, led before she was married
(or so one leaf of what's left would have it)
to the dark bedroom of Persephone, for so long
nowhere at home, either here or there, forever
returning and falling back again
into the dark of these ten thousand years?
The train leaps toward Italy; words fall away
through the dark into the dark bedroom
of everything left behind, the unendingness
of things lost track of—of who, of where—
where I'm losing track of language.

LET THE AIR CIRCULATE

spaces between
archetypal openings   the aperture
seen through binoculars   carved by the lone boatman's
arm athwart the tiller   the schooner's traveling
house of air   split like a nutshell   or a bivalve's domicile
jalousies   belfries   cupolas   floor-through
apartments   let the air circulate   spaces between (sixteen
floors up and still rising)   scaffolded pourers
of reinforced concrete   by the motorized   wheelbarrowful
silhouetted   (a hardhatted frieze)   make of them
something unwittingly classical

clamdiggers
wading mudflats   bending in attitudes
older than   the names of anything   spaces between
things looked at   or unlooked at   beatitudes
of the unaware they're   being looked at
eiders flying   straight as a die   to wherever they're going
triglyph and metope   of air   let the light pass
let the air circulate   let there be intervals
for moving   apart   for
coming back together

the antipodal
the antiphonal   the gradual
the totally unexpected   the counted on   as infallible
the look of   from a particular   window
an island   in profile
the fish-spine   silhouette   of a particular
spruce   intersecting at nightfall   the unaltering interval
of 'Tit Manan light   opening up   folding into
itself   fading   brightening   an orbiting
sidereal buttercup

from ARCHAIC FIGURE

(1987)

ARCHAIC FIGURE

Headless in East Berlin, no goddess
but a named mere girl (Ornithe, "Little Bird")
out of the rubble, six centuries underneath
    the plinth of what we quaintly call

Our Time, informs the foaming underside
of linden boulevards in bloom, sweet hide
laid open onto—sterile as an operating table,
    past the closed incision of the Wall—

the treeless reach of Alexanderplatz,
paved counterpart of the interior flatland,
halfway across the globe, we'd left behind:
    projection, factor, yield, the quantifiable

latitude; malls, runways, blacktop; tressed
cornsilk and alfalfa, drawn milk of the humdrum
nurture there were those of us who ran away from
    toward another, earlier, bonier

one, another middle of the earth, yearned-
for stepmotherland of Hölderlin and Goethe:
sunlight and grief, the cypress and the
    crucifix, the vivid poverty

of terraced slopes, of bread, wine, olives,
fig and pomegranate shade we stumbled into,
strolling the sad northern drizzle, in
    the uprooted Turks' quasi-bazaar,

as here, among uprooted artifacts, we've come
upon this shape's just-lifted pleats, her
chitoned stillness the cold chrism of a time
    that saw—or so to us it seems—

with unexampled clarity to the black core
of what we are, of everything we were to be,
have since become. Who stands there headless.
    Barbar, she would have called us all.

THE OLIVE GROVES OF THASOS

Thronging the warped treadmill
of antiquity, the silver-polled
assemblies, knothole-
tunneled, generations-old

abeyances, posthumous postures
and contortions of a common
weathering, their burled stupor
pierced and cloven

by fierce threnodies of
daybreak, penetrable,
root-cooled in dazzlements
of unquarried marble,

these wards of turbulence
beneath the shaken
shrines of the acropolis,
delivering a gray-green

annual glut of worry-
beads that blacken
in October, after the summer
people have all gone,

when from the villages along
the shore, where in the evenings
we watched the fishing
boats go out in strings

of three, in trinities,
from each of whose sterns
there bloomed a mimic
trinity of lanterns,

linked in a ring, as
darkness fell, to frame
a single, cyclic reënactment
of the timeless; and from

the plane-tree-dimmed, cool-
all-summer refuge
of hill villages above the
tideline of gray foliage;

from the middle villages
the buses pass through, their
hens, their dust and oleanders,
their voluble cafés no more

than islets in the vast,
single surf of olive
groves that circumscribe,
that are the chief live-

lihood and artifact of
Thasos—the whole populace
turns out, with tarpaulins and
poles, to bring in the harvest

of these trees: of this time-gnarled
community of elders—so many-
shaped, so warped, so densely
frugal, so graceful a company,

what more can we say, we who have
seen the summer boats go out,
tasted the dark honey, and savored
the oil-steeped, black, half-bitter fruit?

TEMPE IN THE RAIN

What leaf-fringed legend haunts
this sodden loess of picnics,
sardine-tin litter dripped on
by unmythic fig and laurel—
what latterday pursuits,
      what struggle

to escape the tourist traps,
what souvenir-stall
indignities beside the
footbridge, what coffee bar
depopulated by a sudden
      summer downpour?

To this running anachronism,
the giggling, gray-green
roar that fills a gorge
(sweet Thames! run softly)
old books refer to as the
      vale of Tempe,

the tributaries writhe,
sidle, and defy connection
with the roadside spring, high
up, at which two days ago the
bus made an unscheduled
      stop (we

all got out, washed fruit, filled
bottles, drank from our hands,
found a marsh-marigold in
bloom) or with, above the plain
of Thessaly (Peneus shimmering
      like the Python

Apollo slew, and having slain,
fled here to undo the pollution)
the crazy pinnacles of silt
compacted, cracked open, rain-
and-wind-sanded, where hermit
      monks hole up in

precarious balconies aswarm with
reptilian slitherings, with
gilding, martyrdoms and demons,
with the bong of bells to deafen
and the smell of flame-warmed
      beeswax to sweeten

a side trip Spenser never
contemplated; nor did Keats,
on whose account I've just
jumped off the bus, in this
unseasonable summer rain, to
      find no trace

here of Apollo in pursuit,
mad for the green, leaf-
slippery virginity of Daphne,
but rather, in a hollow under
Mount Olympus' obliviously
      pagan shoulder,

this shrine warmed by a
fragrant sweat of brown beeswax—
where, since some memorial
piety seems called for, before
the ikon of another virgin,
      I've lit a taper.

THERMOPYLAE

Where the bay flashed, and an unrecorded number
of the Persian troops, whip-flicked into the spear-
clogged hourglass of the pass, were impaled and fell
screaming from the precipice to drown, the mirror

clogs: geography too gathers dust, though busloads
of us (sandaled Germans mostly), hankering for
an attar or a foothold, a principle that still
applies, a cruse of oil, a watershed no rain erodes,

find small inkling of what was staved off here,
or saved. A calcined stillness, beehives, oleanders,
polluted air, the hung crags livid; on the little hill
(beneath, the bay flashed as men fell and went under

screaming) where a stone lion once stood in honor
of that grade-school byword of a troop commander
Leonidas, we ponder a funneled-down inscription: Tell
them for whom we came to kill and were killed, stranger,

how brute beauty, valor, act, air, pride, plume here
buckling, guttered: closed in from behind, our spears
smashed, as, the last defenders of the pass, we fell,
we charged like tusked brutes and gnawed like bears.

LEAVING YÁNNINA

The lake like glass, like space
framed in a verdigris of reeds:
the arrow-pointed threadpulls
of small boats that scarcely
flaw the surface,
the mosque a floating
waterlily-garden of the air
upended on a minaret.
                 Last night
as, thrusting past the public square,
the strut of a platoon in khaki
cut through the burble and
meander of the *volta*,
the warm whiff, from
souvlaki stalls, of burning meat
took on a hint of carnage.
                 This morning
in the little archeological museum, time
lies still: the earrings,
the arrowpoints, the spearheads
no one will ever flee again
through time
or space: some latent source
stands open like a room.

MEDUSA

The tentacles, the brazen phiz whose glare
stands every fibril of the mind on end—
lust looked at backward as it were,
an antique scare tactic, either self-protection
or a libel on the sex whose periodic
blossom hangs its ungathered garland
from the horned clockwork of the moon:
as cause or consequence, or both, hysteric
symptoms no doubt figure here. She'd been
a beauty till Poseidon, in a flagrant
trespass, closed with her on Athena's temple floor.

The tide-rip torrents in the blood, the dark
gods not to be denied—or a mere indiscretion?
Athena had no time at all for talk like this.
The sea-god might be her old rival, but the woman
he'd gone to bed with was the one who paid.
A virginal revenge at one remove—there's none more
sordid or more apt to ramify, as this one did:
the fulgent tresses roiled to water-snake-
like writhe, and for long lashes'
come-hither flutterings, the stare
that hardens the psyche's soft parts to rock.

The female ogre, for the Puritan
revisionists who took her over, had a new
and siren sliminess. John Milton
put her at the gate of hell, *a woman to
the waist, and fair; but ended foul, in
many a scaly fold, voluminous and vast*—
whose name indeed was Sin. And in the den
of doctrine run amok, the armored glister
of a plodding Holiness revealed her
as likewise divided but, all told, *most
loathsome, filthy, foul, and full of vile disdain.*

The Gorgon, though, is no such Manichean tease,
no mantrap caterer of forbidden dishes,
whose lewd stews keep transgression warm.
The stinging jellyfish, the tubeworm,
the tunicate, the sea anemone's
whorled comb are privier to her mysteries:
her salts are cold, her home-
land Hyperborean (the realm that gave us
the Snow Queen and the English gentleman),
her mask the ravening aspect of the moon,
her theater a threshing floor that terror froze.

Terror of origins: the sea's heave, the cold mother
of us all; disdain of the allure that draws us in,
that stifles as it nurtures, that feeds on
what it feeds, on what it comforts, whether male
or female: ay, in the very tissue of desire
lodge viscid barbs that turn the blood to coral,
the heartbeat to a bed of silicates. What surgeon
can unthread those multiplicities of cause
of hurt from its effect; dislodge, spicule by spicule,
the fearful armories within; unclench the airless
petrifaction toward the core, the geode's rigor?

PERSEUS

His errand took him to the brink of Ragnarok,
past the last pillar of the charted world, where rain-
worn prototypes of animals and men,
extinct long since, preserved the evidence
of rookeries whose motive force went dark,
sealed shut by that grimace: eroded
stumps of horror antedating even
Odysseus, for whom the Gorgon's head
harrowed with unmanning fear the corridors
of Tartarus, that feeding trough of nightmares,
where every look breeds dread: unstared-down landmark,
last, first and most primitive of portents.

He came armed with an adamantine kris
Hermes had lent him, plus certain items gotten
(as so often happens when crusading zeal
sets forth) by means not over nice: prodigious
sandals' heavier-than-air device, the cowl
of a purloined intelligence, the pouch of blackmail
extorted from the Graeae, a triplet sisterhood
tied to an economy of scarcity (one tooth and one
eye among them, intercepted as they slid
from hand to hand); and above all indispensable,
the shield Athena gave, whose burnished metal
served as an intervening mirror of the Gorgon.

Like any other prospector for the hard,
the heavy, the hideously toxic,
he knew the risk he ran: he could not look
except at one remove at what he'd vowed to take
and hustle out: that head, struck
bleeding from its trunk, whose clotted
dreadlocks and gagged, staring scowl became
the badge and totem of what no one can
encounter and survive: among dredged glisten-
ings of seaweed, the unfledged millennium—
the branched, ineradicable stem of time,
whose cold coils wind about the moon's inexorable clock.

And even as he fled, the undiplomatic
pouchful safely stowed, two angry other
Gorgons in pursuit (as any Greek will caution,
mischiefs tend to come in triplicate),
the stem he'd lopped, already pregnant by Poseidon,
gave birth to Chrysaor, precocious warrior
whose cumbering falchion would overhang
the ungrazed field, the unturned furrow of the future,
and to unbridled Pegasus, the winged fraternal twin
who kicked at Helicon, and from whose hoofprint sprung
the mirror flash among the cromlechs—one wet
eyeblink in the antediluvial dark.

HIPPOCRENE

I came to the puddle. I could not cross it. Identity failed me.
We are nothing, I said, and fell.

VIRGINIA WOOLF, The Waves

The cold spring
of an intense depression,
moon-horror-struck posthumous
offspring of Medusa,
harbinger of going under,
of death by water.

Though above the pillars
of ruined Sounion the air
is calm, the white-lipped,
violet-hued flowerbed
of drowning, fraying
at the rim,

lies sleek with signals
of unbeing: the cold hoofprint's
doorway into nothing
metamorphosing from a
puddle in a courtyard,
the huge irruption

of blank seas the psyche
cannot cross: the terror-
twinning muse, the siren
and the solace: done and
undone by water—whether
beyond the stormy

Hebrides, the voyage
out, the long-looked-forward-to
excursion to the lighthouse:
the Ouse closing over;
a fin, far out. The waves
break on the shore.

ATHENA

Force of reason, who shut up the shrill
foul Furies in the dungeon of the Parthenon,
led whimpering to the cave they live in still,

beneath the rock your city foundered on:
who, equivocating, taught revenge to sing
(or seem to, or be about to) a kindlier tune:

mind that can make a scheme of anything—
a game, a grid, a system, a mere folder
in the universal file drawer: uncompromising

mediatrix, virgin married to the welfare
of the body politic: deific contradiction,
warbonnet-wearing olive-bearer, author

of the law's delays, you who as talisman
and totem still wear the aegis, baleful
with Medusa's scowl (though shrunken

and self-mummified, a Gorgon still): cool
guarantor of the averted look, the guide
of Perseus, who killed and could not kill

the thing he'd hounded to its source, the dread
thing-in-itself none can elude, whose counter-
feit we halfway hanker for: aware (gone mad

with clarity) we have invented all you stand for,
though we despise the artifice—a space to savor
horror, to pre-enact our own undoing in—
living, we stare into the mirror of the Gorgon.

PERSEUS AIRBORNE

. . . Thereafter, Perseus was driven by warring winds all over
the vast expanse of sky. . . . Three times he saw the frozen
north, three times, borne southwards, he beheld the claws of the
Crab. . . .

OVID, *Metamorphoses, Book IV*
(TRANSLATED BY MARY M. INNES)

What lay beyond those blowing beaches,
that heaving barrier, was still unmapped:
the wind-scoured moors of Patagonia,
the blizzard whiteouts of the Antarctic,

vast scarfed screechings at the center
of a Caribbean air mass; the norther,
the chinook, El Niño; gale force in wait,
the lurking possibility of wind shears:

even for a son of Zeus the Thunderer
(who'd impregnated his mother Danaë,
in a daring raid, with pollen-gold),
to be airborne entails a daunting,

a radical insouciance. The B-52s
panting in tandem, not-quite-new-fangled
coursers of the Sun, howl up from grasslands
that were terra incognita once: beyond

the last temptation, the untaken leap
they now rehearse, rehearse, rehearse.

ATLAS IMMOBILIZED

Hulk grown monumental with refusal,
intolerable landlock under the stars
he cannot shift, cannot rescind, cannot
look up into the cave of—

delirium, myopic rockface, the towering
quagmires of infinity
shrunk to a hairshirt—
what ultimatum

binds this certitude upon his back
that once set in place, nothing can alter?
Is even the moon's seeming to loiter,
a half-hearted voyeur,

mere robotry? The wedding party
garroted inside the skull, the
psyche's well-heeled, wall-
to-wall captivity,

the conversation pit a desert: airborne
murder overhead in squadroned
follicles, mad seed of the
purely theoretical,

orbiting as talks continue, with the usual
handwringing: thrones, dominations, powers
adhering to the same unshakable
proposition: nothing

truly is except what overcomes. No
rapprochement: the moon looks in,
moves off again: Orion's
mitered studs once more

abrade the hemisphere. Are all these
rigors fixed, the single step
untakable, the postures of the
conversation pit unfree

to bend, to make amends? Were all
that's still locked up in fright
to shriek, might not some warden, even
yet, unforge the key?

GEORGE ELIOT COUNTRY

For Gordon Haight (1901–1985)

From this Midland scene—glum slagheaps,
barge canals, gray sheep, the vivid overlap
of wheatfield and mustard hillside like
out-of-season sunshine, the crabbed silhouette
of oak trees (each joint a knot, each knot
a principled demurral—tough, arthritic, stubborn
as the character of her own father)—fame,
the accretion of a Pyrrhic happiness, had
exiled her to London, with its carriages
and calling cards, its screaming headaches.

Griff House—dear old Griff, she wistfully
apostrophized it—in those days still intact,
its secrets kept, has now been grafted to a
motel-cum-parking-lot beside the trunk road,
whose raw, ungainly seam of noise cuts through
the rainy solace of Griff Lane: birdsong,
coal smoke, the silvered powderings of
blackthorn, a flowering cherry tree's
chaste flare; the sludge-born, apoplectic
screech of jet aircraft tilting overhead.

The unmapped sources that still fed nostalgia
for a rural childhood survive the witherings
of retrospect: the look of brickyards,
stench of silk mills, scar of coal mines,
the knife of class distinction: wall-enclosed,
parkland-embosomed, green-lawned Arbury Hall,
fan-vaulting's stately fakeries, the jewel-
stomachered, authentic shock of Mary Fitton and
her ilk portrayed, the view of fishponds—school
and role model of landed-proprietary England.

Born in the year of Peterloo, George Eliot
had no illusions as to the expense of such
emoluments. Good society (she wrote), floated
on gossamer wings of light irony, required no less

than an entire, arduous national existence,
condensed into unfragrant, deafening factories,
cramped into mines, sweating at furnaces, or
scattered in lonely houses on the clayey or chalky
cornland . . . where Maggie Tulliver, despairing
of gentility, ran off to join the gypsies.

Violets still bloom beside the square-towered
parish church where Mary Anne was christened;
the gashed nave of Coventry fills up with rain
(another howling doodlebug of fright hurls itself
over); the church from which, refusing to commit
the fiction of a lost belief in One True Body,
she stayed away, upholds the fabric in which her
fictions, perdurable now, cohere like fact: Lydgate
still broods, Grandcourt still threatens, and
in Mrs. Transome disappointment turns to stone.

HIGHGATE CEMETERY

Laid in unconsecrated ground, a scandal
still—note how good Gerard Hopkins
recoiled from what a queer, awkward girl,
frail-shouldered, massive, rickety,
volcanic, out of an unconsecrated
attachment, a marriage that was
no marriage (one would have added,
till opprobrium intervened, *but
something better*) to a pockmarked
lightweight of a drama critic,
saw blossom: this domestic improbability,
this moonflower: they were happy.

Happiness: *that*—as it always has been—
was the scandal. As for the uninhibited
pursuit of same, gone merrily
amok, by now, among the lit-up
purlieus of a game show (died
of a conniption, beaming): time
spared her that, though not the cold shoulder,
the raw east wind, fog, the roar that issues
from the other side of silence; not headache,
kidney stone, the ravages of cancer—or
of grief foreseen, met with, engulfed by,
just barely lived through.

Nature (she'd written, years before) *repairs
her ravages, but not all. The hills
underneath their green vestures bear
the marks of past rending.* Johnny Cross,
younger by two decades, a banker,
athletic, handsome, read Dante with her,
fell in love; repeatedly, distressingly,
spoke of marriage, was at last accepted.
Another scandal—in the eyes of devotees
who looked on marrying at all with horror
as for the breathing fishbowl of appearances.

Grotesque, my dear. An episode in Venice,
on their honeymoon (who knows what makes any
of us do what we do?) was somehow weathered.
Then, in six months, she was dead.

At Highgate, the day she was buried,
a cold rain fell, mixed with snow. Slush
underfoot. Mud tracked inside the chapel.
Her brother Isaac, more than twenty years estranged
(a ravage never healed), was there
among the mourners—hordes of them,
the weather notwithstanding. Edith Simcox,
crazed with devotion to this woman who'd been,
in her ill-favored way, so beautiful, arrived
with a nosegay of violets, wandered off distracted
into the dusk, came to herself finally
at a station she didn't recognize,
somewhere in Hampstead.

In rain-wet May, not quite a century later—
cow parsley head-high, the unkempt
walks a blur, faint drip of birdsong,
ivy taking over—the stone is hard to find.
Herbert Spencer, a creature of exemplary
good sense, however ill-equipped
for rapture, lies buried not far off,
his monumental neighbor a likeness
of Karl Marx, egregious in granite—
godfather of such looked-for victories
over incorrigible Nature, his memory red
with nosegays ribboned in Chinese.

GRASMERE

For Lois Squires

Rainstorms that blacken like a headache
where mosses thicken, and the mornings
smell of jonquils, the stillness
of hung fells thronged with the primaveral
noise of waterfalls—contentment
pours in spate from every slope; the lake fills,
the kingcups drown, and still it rains,
the sheep graze, their black lambs bounce
and skitter in the wet: such weather
one cannot say, here, why
one is still so happy.

Cannot say, except it's both so wild
and so tea-cozy cozy, so snugly
lush, so English.

A run-into-the-ground complacency nonetheless
is given pause here. At Dove Cottage
dark rooms bloom with coal fires; the backstairs
escape hatch into a precipitous small orchard
still opens; bedded cowslips, primroses,
fritillaries' checkered, upside-down
brown tulips still flourish where
the great man fled the neighbors:
a crank ("Ye torrents, with
your strong and constant voice, protest
the wrong," he cried—i.e., against the Kendal-
to-Windermere railway). By middle age a Tory,
a somewhat tedious egotist even (his wild
oats sown abroad) when young: "He cannot," his sister
had conceded, "be so pleasing as my
fondness makes him"—a coda
to the epistolary cry, "Oh Jane
the last time we were together he
won my affection . . ." What gives one
pause here—otherwise one might not
care, as somehow one does,

for William Wordsworth—
is Dorothy.

"Wednesday. . . . He read me his poem. After dinner
he made a pillow of my shoulder—I read to him
and my Beloved slept."

The upstairs bedroom where the roof leaked
and the chimney smoked, the cool buttery
where water runs, still voluble, under the flagstones;
the room she settled into after his marriage
to Mary Hutchinson, and shared with, as
the family grew, first one, then
two of the children; the newsprint
she papered it with for warmth (the circle
of domestic tranquillity cannot
guard her who sleeps single
from the Cumbrian cold) still legible:
such was the dreamed-of place, so long
too much to hope for. "It was in winter
(at Christmas) when he was last at Forncett,
and every day as soon as we rose from dinner
we used to pace the gravel in the Garden
till six o'clock." And this,
transcribed for Jane alone from
one of William's letters: "Oh, my dear, dear Sister
with what transport shall I again
meet you, with what rapture . . ." The orphan
dream they'd entertained, that she had named
The Day of My Felicity: to live
together under the same roof,
in the same house. Here,
at Dove Cottage.

"A quiet night. The fire flutters, and
the watch ticks. I hear nothing else
save the breathing of my Beloved . . ."

Spring, when it arrived again, would bring
birch foliage filmy as the bridal veil
she'd never wear; birds singing; the sacred stain
of bluebells on the hillsides; fiddleheads
uncoiling in the brakes, inside each coil
a spine of bronze, pristinely hoary;
male, clean-limbed ash trees whiskered
with a foam of pollen; bridelike
above White Moss Common, a lone wild cherry
candle-mirrored in the pewter of the lake.
On March 22nd—a rainy day, with William
very poorly—resolves were made
to settle matters with Annette, in France,
and that he should go to Mary. On the 27th,
after a day fraught with anxiety, a morning
of divine excitement: At breakfast
William wrote part of an ode. It was
the *Intimations.*

The day after, they took the excitement to Coleridge
at Keswick, arriving soaked to the skin. There, after dinner,
she had one of her headaches.

A bad one's ghastly worst, the packed ganglion's
black blood clot: The Day of My Felicity
curled up inside a single sac with its
perfidious twin, the neurasthenic
nineteenth-century housemate
and counterpart of William's incorrigibly
nervous stomach: "I do not know from what
cause it is," he wrote, "but during
the last three years I have never
had a pen in my hand five minutes
before my whole frame becomes a bundle
of uneasiness." To ail, here in this place,
this hollow formed as though to be the vessel
of contentment—of sweet mornings

smelling of jonquils, of tranquillity
at nightfall, of habitual strolls
along the lakeshore, among the bracken
the old, coiled-up agitation
glistening: birds singing, the greening
birches in their wedding veils,
the purple stain of bluebells:

attachment's uncut knot—so rich, so dark,
so dense a node the ache still bleeds,
still binds, but cannot speak.

COLEORTON

Again, at evening, the winter walks
supported on her brother's arm—not,
as at Forncett, snatched, fugitive,
but an entitlement, an earned dependency,
the welding of everything somehow since
lived through: her brother's wedding day,
those vows whose undertow was of such force
it laid her prostrate on an unfamiliar bed:
Mary, her sister now, delivered
of three babies—"all famous," declares
their father, who can be a wag, can
quite well write a letter when he chooses,
"for being exceedingly ill-managed":
sweet, stolid, vengeful Johnny; Dora,
a tireless chatterer; and poor Thomas, in
the midst of teething, who cries and cries:
three safe lyings-in, cut through by one
fearful bereavement: washed ashore
weeks after the *Abergavenny* foundered,
the body of John Wordsworth lies
in Wyke churchyard, on the Dorset coast. No stone
marks it. Two years will soon have passed.
They have not gone there. At Grasmere,
every gale that shudders in the chimneys
is his memorial—made the more poignant
by months, night after night, of worrying
over Coleridge.
                         Whom they await here,
while the forebodings thicken: worse,
yes, worse even than their brother's shipwreck
(though that has left her shrunken, pitiful
and old at thirty-five—"They tell me,"
she writes, "I have never looked so well
in my life. This *I* do not believe"), the shock
of Coleridge returned from Malta,
bloated, despondent, sodden. The ruined
landmarks of dependency mere breath,

oneself a leaf, a weak vine lifted, dandled,
dropped: the poet's whimper of "There is
a change, and I am poor": to be deprived
for life of what not even she, whose shoulder
he'd made a pillow of, after the labor,
the lying-in of genius: a genius unstable,
!arge, of little note, sneered at
by the reviewers: deprived of what
not even she can any longer offer! This it is
that throbs between them like an abscess
as they pace, at evening, below
Coleorton Hall.
                      His altered look:
the gray-eyed luminary of the day,
not quite a decade since he first,
leaping that stream, had been admitted
to the startled core of their attachment,
now sunk in fat: the stillborn squalor
of their late reunion, the meeting he'd
repeatedly eluded, more charged with dread
than the stark loss of John, so wholly
to be depended on, so blameless.
Without blame, only an overweening,
hurt solicitude, they wait for him
to end the maundering requitals, the
evasions of an ending, and quit the ruin
that is his marriage; while the hum
and tremor of a blander tie, the bondage
of a new endearment, is entered on
with Lady Beaumont, whom they're beholden to
for this lent space, these walks at evening,
the unobstructed sunsets of which at Grasmere,
"shut up as we are in our deep valley,
we have but a glimpse. . . . On Wednesday evening,
my Brother and I walked backwards and forwards
under the trees . . . until the sky
was all over gloomy, and two lights
(we supposed from coal-pits) were left to shine . . .

I have kept back from speaking of Coleridge,
for what can I say? . . ."
                          They wait.
The Poem of Her Brother's Life, that portico
to the unbuilt cathedral of his mind—"divine"
had been the word set down by Coleridge himself
that day when, listening high among the tarns,
he'd felt the lintel of it soar, heard an
entire design reverberate—that prelude
to a greater undertaking waits. Turned
landscape architect meanwhile, her brother
charts for his patron a winter garden
"which shall present no image of chillness,
decay or desolation when the face of nature
everywhere is cold, decayed or desolate. . . .
We never" (he continues) "pass in our evening walk
the cluster of holly bushes . . . but we unsettle
a number of small birds which have taken shelter
there. . . . The whole Bush seems aflutter. . . ."
His mind wanders backward into summer, to a time
when what had seemed the idyl of dependency
rushed into blossom: "I never saw so beautiful
a shrub as one tall holly . . . near a house
we occupied" (another house not theirs—
how many since those winter walks at Forncett,
the scene of their resolve to live together
under one roof!) "in Somersetshire:
it was attired with woodbine, and upon
the very tip of the topmost bough
'that looked out at the sky' " (a tremor
here—fallacious pathos of the one
red leaf, last of its clan, that dances
topmost) "was one large honeysuckle flower,
like a star. . . ."
                    They wait. Together,
as the older stars come into bloom
above the coal-pits, they look up
and feel the prospect darken.

RYDAL MOUNT

"Now, I must tell you of our grandeur,"
she'd written. "We are going to have
a *Turkey*!!! carpet in the dining room . . .
You stare . . . 'Are they changed, are they
setting up for fine Folk . . . ?' " Yes,

they were changed. One year had seen
comic, crippled Catharine, aged three,
and Thomas, of whom much had been expected,
both laid in Grasmere churchyard; then
their father, already gray and elderly

at just past forty, set in a position:
Distributor of Stamps for Westmorland,
canvasser for the Lowthers, who all but
owned Penrith ("Sad, sad, sad," radical
John Keats would mutter, passing through).

Soon she'd be caught up with him in all
the brouhaha of a bought election. Yes,
there had been a change: De Quincey, so
lately of their household, so innocently
besotted with Catharine, married now

to opium and the simple girl he'd gotten
a bastard by. "Ruined," D. pronounced. And
paid no more visits. From Dove Cottage—
the talk there, the incandescent silences
beside the fire ("I hear nothing else save

the breathing of my Beloved")—indeed
there was a change. Her brother wrote
now, grandly, of Mutability, of outward
forms (unspecified) that melt away
like hoarfrost. Surprised by joy (he wrote),

he'd turned to share the transport—turned
to whom but Catharine, with a sublimity
he could no more come down from than she,
poor mite, in life could walk upright. Aloft
at such an eminence, he'd grown more craggy;

nobody argued with him; much wifely tact
was spent, a whole household of amanuenses
circled him on tiptoe. Reputation sealed in,
spicule by spicule, the old sore wounds—
grief, ridicule, the worm of conscience:

Annette and Caroline, the larger work undone.
Word came that Coleridge was dead. "A long
sit with knitting on my knee," his sister
noted in her diary. Words for the chill
he felt came more slowly: *power frozen*

at its marvellous source . . . Our haughty
life is crowned with darkness, like London
with its own black wreath. There had been
great alteration: that was the year
his sister—the ruin of her youth beset

by mass defections from within the body,
the firebrand of her old vivacity half-
quenched, a hutch of glowworms—in flight
from grandeur, vicissitude, fine Folk,
took refuge in the nunnery of madness.

Fits of verse, poured out from memory.
Churchwardens mocked. Unseemly noises.
Outbursts. Children and strangers kept away.
Small, shrunken, wild-eyed, she'd command
whoever came into the room to stir the fire.

There would be remissions. "News—news,"
she'd write. "I must seek for news. My
own thoughts are a wilderness . . . The
laburnum with its naked seedpods shivers. . . ."
"Stir the fire!" Her brother, poet laureate

since Southey died, obeys her, sits here
with her, watching: a doddering pair, like
gypsies camping out, the way they'd camped
one night at Tintern, the untended grandeurs
of a time gone dim gone dim behind them.

AN ANATOMY OF MIGRAINE

In memory of Annette Leo

I

Inquire what consciousness is made of
with Galen, with Leonardo, Leeuwenhoek
or Dr. Tulp, and you find two hemispheres,
    a walnut in a bath of humors,

a skullcapped wreath of arteries, a weft
of fibrous thoroughfares along the walls
of Plato's cave, the cave walls of Lascaux:
    those shambling herds, this hollow

populous with fissures, declivities,
arboreal thicketings, with pairings
and degrees, this fist-sized flutter,
    mirror-lake of matter,

seat of dolor and jubilee, the law of Moses
and the giggling underneath the bedclothes,
of Bedlam and the Coronation Anthem—all
    these shut up in a nutshell.

Go back, step past the nadir of whatever
happened to divide our reckoning, a fraction
of an anti-millennium, a millennium and more
    ago, and hear Hippocrates declare

the brain is double. Since then, as to
where, in these paired hemispheres, the self—
with its precarious sense of *I am I,*
    with its extremes of possibility—

resides, we've come no nearer than
Descartes, who thought he'd found it in
the pineal teardrop. (Now no one's sure
    what that gland is for.)

Inquire what consciousness is made of
of Simone Weil, and she answers: Pain.
The drag of gravity. The sledge of time.
    A wretchedness no system

can redeem, extreme affliction that
destroys the *I;* nothing is worse, she
wrote. And knew whereof she wrote, who'd
    drudged, with an ineptitude

only the saints would find becoming,
in a Renault assembly line; had seen
the waste, how small the profit, how
    many suffer and learn nothing, how,

as Kate Croy observed (and chose accordingly),
deprivation made people selfish, left them
robbed of the last rags of character,
    preyed and put upon, enmired in rancor.

She'd seen, was not immune, had been there;
had her own cliffs of fall within the skull:
headache, driven by whose cringing thud
    she'd scrupulously noted

a craven urge within herself to cause
someone, anyone, to suffer likewise.
Is the mind divided, as Hippocrates
    declared the brain is?

Did she invite in what all but unhinged her?
She'd known well-being, however threaded
with crevasses; been witness to the white
    stars' stillness overhead, the white

drift of petals from the apple trees: such
tranquil spanglings of the retina of time,

she could not doubt the universe
    is full, that splendors

of entity, of grace past meeting face
to face, project, each one, its fearful
opposite, its double—as each electron
    in the universe its Manichaean

anti-particle: in every molecule of
every nerve cell, such forces within
forces within forces, the marvel
    is that anyone is ever well,

that consciousness is ever other than
a frazzled buzz, one long sick headache.
My father never gave the name of migraine
    to that locked-in retribution

of the self against—against who knows
what or whom? Fenced brutes, barbed wire
and rawhide, fear of a father's anger,
    mere heredity? His father,

to a grandchild seemingly so mild, so
equable, had labored, I would one day
learn, through that same territory:
    days of headache, nights so worry-

racked he thought his mind would go.
Heredity: finally, in a little memoir
impelled by painful rectitude, he'd
    set down how dread

of what had made him made *his* father
by temper hard: got out of wedlock,
the old conundrum—*Who am I? where did
    I come from?*—twice riddled,

learning whose bastard he was, he'd
manfully assumed that surname. Stirred
or unstirred, the generations' cesspool
    fills; the circle of the wrathful,

ventilated, usurps the crawl space:
all Hell's hand-me-downs hung from
the spindle of Necessity, each sprung-
    from-two, spun-out-of-nothing

being crying from within, *I, I,*
while time that bears the thinking
being toward what it cannot bear
    impales it here.

    2

Here is impaled—hinge, mirror-image,
cleft, and crossing-place—the hard
world-knot of entity, the One not one
    at all but contradiction,

Nohow and Contrariwise, chiasmus through
the looking-glass: fraternal inter-
twinings, at the very core a battle;
    so the neurobiological

dilemma of the paired, the hemispheric,
re-ramifies—bright, dark; left, right;
right, wrong—and so euphoria gives way to
    spleen, its obverse, as though

the cosmos repented of itself, of all those
promises, all those placebos: the sun-flooded
square, stone blossoming, each canvas seen as
    a live aperture, a space

to step into; then the usual consequence,
of waking to another migraine: three days
in a darkened room, the drastic easement
    of ergot, derivative of poisoned

rye long known to midwives, proscribed for
her too fragile bloodways. (Lift the hem
of medicine, and you discover torture
    and placebo twinned, still there.)

No cure. This happened, was set down.
I read the manuscript amazed. We hadn't met.
Letters had been exchanged, her driven,
    bannered penmanship an

army out of *Alexander Nevsky*—the whips,
the wolves, the keening steppes, the Russian
mother-lap her history had been torn from.
    One day a parcel came,

impeccably hand-wrapped, inside it an
uncrafted something—three sea-winnowed
sandstones, a wave-buffed driftwood elbow—
    from the beach at Malibu.

I blushed, both flattered and adroitly
remonstrated with: the manuscript (so many
women writing books, their scripts unread,
    still hoping for some recognition!) I'd

said I'd look at not yet opened. I opened
it that day—though not before an ounce
of Maine-coast beach glass had been
    wrapped and sent, transcon-

tinental reciprocity—and read it through.
The migraine on the day she was to fly

to Italy, a frame and a foreshadow
  of that volatile chiaroscuro,

a life repeatedly, strenuously, just barely
put back in order—that migraine (*You too!*)
set her instantly, for me, with an elite
  vised by the same splenic coronet:

Dorothy Wordsworth, George Eliot, Margaret
Fuller, Marx, Freud, Tolstoy, Chopin, Lewis
Carroll, Simone Weil, Virginia Woolf:
  a gathering of shades, of

forebears and best friends who'd all gone
to that hard school. Since Homer peered
at Tartarus, we've looked into a gazetteer-
  authenticated Hell, a place for

meeting with—for hearing yet again the
voices of—the dead. The cosmos, looped with
bigfoot odysseys set down in moon dust, now
  gives it no place but in the hollow

of the skull: that Amazon where no explorer
goes except on hands and knees, the strait
last entrance to the fields of asphodel
  where, say, Simone Weil

and Virginia Woolf might meet and find no distance,
after all, in what they'd finally perceived—
what the latter wrote of as " 'reality' . . . beside
  which nothing matters"; she who'd,

at moments, bridged the mind's crevasse: "Lying
in bed, mad, & seeing the sunlight quivering, like
gold water, on the wall, I've heard the voices of the
  dead here, and felt, through it all, exquisitely

happy." Anny, friend by mail, what I would give
for time to talk of this! We met just once; at ease
at once, walked barefoot on the sands at Malibu,
    the blue air that afternoon, by

some semantic miracle, angelic; picked up stones,
observed the dolphins. A last letter, in that script
her unemphatic beauty stanched without a trace.
    Then, in a hand I did not recognize—

cramped, small, precise—one from the husband
who'd survived her: dead in her sleep. No
warning. But she'd known, had written of, in
    one half-retracted note, a premonition.

I miss her. Though our two lives just touched,
the torn fabric of some not-yet-imagined
prospect hangs there, streamered, splendid,
    vague: well-being rainbowed

over a lagoon of dark: all that I'm even
halfway sure of marked by that interior cleft
(black, white; sweet, sour; adazzle, dim), I
    live with shades of possibility,

with strangers, friends I never spoke to, with
the voices of the dead, the sunlight like gold
water on the wall—electron-charged, precarious—
    all tenuously made of consciousness.

ALICE

For an Oxford don, doomed during term to sit
night after night at the high table,
the pardon of a little girl afloat
on an unstygian Thames. No Sibyl
gloomed or ranted at the rabbithole
she entered by—a time-obsessed fussbudget
of a rabbit her Virgil—into the hell
her elders were so grandly glum about.

Persephone and Beatrice among the shades,
she showed the monstrous region underground
for what he'd always thought it was:
the screeching shams, the burbled pieties,
the flummoxes and trapdoors of the mind:
all Oxford flattened to a pack of cards.

LONDON INSIDE AND OUTSIDE

Looked back on happily, the ivy-hung,
back-wall-embowered garden of our
pied-à-terre and domicile in Chelsea
seems oddly like some dream of living
halfway down the well that sheltered
Charles Dodgson's Elsie, Lacie
and Tillie—with those geraniums
in urns, that lily-of-the-valley
bed not quite in bloom, those churring
ringdoves, those thrushes murderously
foraging for earthworms: an exterior
so self-contained, a view so inward
that though at night we'd note
faint window-glimmerings eclipsed by ivy,
we seemed to have no neighbors either
to spy on or be spied on by.

Those strolls at dusk, the sidewalks
puddled underfoot, the streetlamps
an aloof processional (a footfall
once or twice, then silence)
at the hour not of the pulling down
of shades but rather of the drawing
in of curtains on their rods, with
an occasional small, to-be-savored
lapse—the glimpse in solitude
of the young woman meditatively
taking off her coat: or of
the table laid, the TV
in the dining room tuned to the news,
a South-Sea-bubble porthole open
on the mysteries of domicile,
of anchorage, of inside-outside!

The night we took the Underground
to Covent Garden, we found the foyer
at the opera a roofed-in waterfall

of crystal, the staircase we sat on
at the interval to eat our ices
carpet-luscious (even to the shod
sole) as a bed of crimson mosses,
the rose-red lampshades erotic
as hothouse hibiscus. Floated
overhead, a firmament of gilt
and turquoise; as that goes dim,
beneath the royal monogram the bell jar
of illusion lifts, and yet again
we're inside-outside: Norina's
rooftop vista (the duenna
furiously knitting) of a hot-bright
Bay of Naples. In the obscurity
of our neck-craning balcony, we
snuggled undetected. Outside there waited
a shivering, rain-speckled exodus among
dark gardens of the inevitable
umbrellas going up.

BABEL ABOARD THE HELLAS
INTERNATIONAL EXPRESS

Border halt, an hour out of Saloniki.
Washrooms already filthy. Corridor
a frisson of peaked caps, red-seaweed
postage-stamp outlandishnesses at a
standoff. *Gastarbeiter* bound for Munich

in a second-class couchette: sad Greek
whose wife is sick (he tells us in
sepulchral German), who can't stop smoking—
a brown, brown-suited man, his runneled
face a map of nicotine. Slaves of caffeine,

we hop down, throng the last-chance café (none
aboard the train, none in Yugoslavia. No
food either. Warned, we've brought aboard
bread, cheese, wine, olives, peaches), stoke
ourselves with swarthy oversweetened coffee

while brown man lays in his own supply
of—what? It's yogurt: five, six, seven
plastic-lidded tublets' curded slime. He
stacks them (and we shudder) on the filthy
floor. We cut cheese. He smokes. He can't

stop smoking. By designation the compartment
is *Nicht Raucher,* ᾽Απαγορεύεται τὸ Κάπνισμα.
Useless to complain. We're sorry for him.
And anyhow there's a fourth occupant, a
brown man too, who seems inscrutable (he might

be Greek, or might not be) and who, without
apology, murkily, incessantly *ist auch ein
Raucher*—though mainly in the corridor.
Dusk. We're moving. We've crossed the border.
We halt again. We're sots and thralls

of Babel and demography. New ghouls
have come aboard. We scare each other,
telling of papers gone astray. We're passing
through a gorge. The lockstep trudge brings in
new hues, new snarls of peaked-cap seaweed,

old mores, old anxieties: our pasteboard
vitals handed over, peered into, returned or
not returned, repeatedly. It's dark outside.
Glimpses of halted freight cars. Someone
flourishing a flashlight walks the track, to spy

out what spies? what contraband? It's coffee,
someone says. They opened up somebody's suitcase
back there, found it packed with kilo bagfuls. Took
them all. Detained the passenger. We're pouring
wine. Trudge, trudge. Visa control again:

passports one by one are handed back. Mine
not among them. Why? Where is it? Ghoul
shrugs. Trapdoor opening—fright, indignation,
fury, sputtered futile questions. Gallantry
between us: "I'll stay with you." "No,

no. You go on to Munich. You know
you must." I don't believe a word of this, of
course. I take a Miltown. Reiterated gusts
of asking why, dire glee of strangers. Next,
Skopje. I'm being brave. I'm not being brave, I am

in fact behaving childishly. Washroom
so filthy you can't squat. No drinking
water either. Worse: it now turns out
I'm not a martyr. The latest peaked-cap
wearer fingers my shoulder bag. I look

and squirm: It's there. Who put it back?
No way of knowing. "I do feel such a fool.
You won't tell anyone? I'll never live it down."
"It might have been some trick of theirs,"
you say, still gallant. Maybe. I doubt it.

The Skopje passengers flood in. "Komplett!
Komplett!" Our brown companions fend them off.
We settle onto our couchettes. Wake in Belgrade.
No coffee. Hawkers of pasty, tasteless pastries.
New hordes crowd aboard. It's Sunday morning.

"Komplett! Komplett!" All Yugoslavia is traveling,
won't be kept out. The kerchiefed proletariat
from Istanbul, who got on back at Nis, may
be deterred, but not the middle class.
A couple and their little boy have joined us—

sad, tight-garbed, stodgy-prosperous.
Their little boy is blind. Their burden,
shared, is our affliction. Salamander-pale,
he sways, croons, laughs convulsively,
is told to hush; whimpers, subsides again

to sea-cave solitudes we can't envision.
At Zagreb they leave us. The crowds are worse.
"Komplett! Komplett!" No use. Disconsolate
brown man whose wife is sick climbs back
onto top berth to sleep—the one last solace.

His untouched yogurt has begun to spill. A mess.
The washrooms are by now a costive-making,
hopeless *cauchemar*. The Serbs, Slovenes,
Croatians, Bosnians, Albanians, who knows what
else, who swarm the corridors, are civil,

appeal to reason, persist, at last prevail.
Stout ruddy woman; lean, fair-haired, ruddy man;
two small dark nondescripts; one human barrel,
chalk-stripe-tailored, curly-brilliantined,
Lech Walesa–mustachioed, jovial: with these,

till Munich, we're to share what space there is.
They speak some common dialect, we're not
sure which. A bag of prunes is passed.
We offer olives. The conversation grows
expansive: we listen in on every syllable,

uncomprehending, entranced. A bottle
circulates: I hesitate, see what it is,
and sip. Stupendous. Not to be missed,
this brew. It burns, it blazes. Anecdote
evolves, extends, achieves a high adagio,

grows confidential, ends in guffaws. O
for a muse of slivovitz, that fiery booze,
to celebrate this Babel, this untranslatable
divertimento all the way to Munich,
aboard a filthy train that's four hours late!

VENICE REVISITED

While the Frenchmen and Flemings abandoned themselves in a
frenzy of wholesale destruction, the Venetians kept their heads.
They knew beauty when they saw it.
          JOHN JULIUS NORWICH, *A History of Venice*

I

Guise and disguise, the mirrorings and masquerades,
brocaded wallowings, ascensions, levitations:
glimmering interiors, beaked motley; the hide-
and-seek of Tintoretto and Carpaccio. From within
walled gardens' green enclave, a blackbird's warble—
gypsy non sequitur out of root-cumbered
terra firma, a mainland stepped from
to this shored-up barge, this Bucintoro
of mirage, of artifice. Outside the noon-dim
dining room, the all-these-years-uninterrupted
sloshing of canals; bagged refuse, ungathered
filth; the unfed cats, still waiting.
                       To breathe again
the faint stink of this place I had not thought to
revisit in this life; to catch, through shutters
half-latched for the siesta, the same glimpse
of a young girl's laundry—a glimpse half-
preternatural, like an encounter with some
evidence of resurrection: re-entering, to swim
above the mild tumuli of San Marco,
that last surreal upwelling of Byzantium,
is also to disinter the vertigo
of the homesteader's wife who, numb
in the face of the undisguised
prospect of the place she'd come to, drove
a post into the yard outside the sodhouse
to have something, she said, to look at.

2

The place they'd come to—treeless, its sole prospect
the watery skin-scurf of reedbeds, of mudflats

cowering shivering in the dark or sweltering
at noon, no place to hide from vertigo—was no
less desolate. They lived at first
dispersed, in dens of osier and wattle,
hemmed by no familiar dolomite, no tree-blurred
watershed to lift the eyes to—the lagoon
a wan presentiment of the great basin's
vastness—a place for a homesteader's wife
to drift and drown, or else to settle and
grow stolid as a driven post in.
                                        Postpiles driven
into the muck of the lagoon—a million-plus of them,
a thousand-plus times over—would one day undergird
the multiplicity of domes, arcades, façades
of variegated marble, stilts for the stupendous
masquerade of history: the Bucintoro
with the Doge afloat, rowed to the cheering
of lubricious throngs, the whimpering
of lutes: a stage set above the windings
of these onetime sloughs, the hidden
thoroughfares obscure and treacherous
as the dim wagon tracks the homesteaders
would inevitably follow into the disguiseless
grassland, the desolation of
the place they'd come to.

        3

Magnificence of guise and disguise, of the given
and the taken: that a body thought to be
that of Saint Mark—Evangelist, witness to
the crime that had then given birth to faith,
subscriber to the possibility of resurrection—
had been brought here from somewhere, is
believed to be historical. Whether the box
they brought it in—the filched cadaver,
the purported-to-be-sacred relic—in fact contained

merely another masquerade, has long since
ceased to matter. Maskers, lovers of shows,
of music, looters who knew beauty when
they saw it, who (while others rampaged,
raped, or merely smashed) made off with
the famous four bronze horses, and much else,
they did know beauty: give them
at least that credit.

                What stolen relics,
sacred or bogus, what odor of sanctity
or of corruption, would the descendants
of the homesteader's wife who drove
that post to keep herself from going
mad, bring home, to furnish and inform
the likewise unhandsomely acquired
terrain she'd come to? What mainland—
if there is a mainland any more for any
emigré's descendants to return to—
can they claim? What's to be said for
their, for our own faltering empire,
our most unserene republic, other
than that while crusaders of our own
rampaged in Asia, one set foot also
on the maskless, indubitable
wasteland of the moon?

MAN FEEDING PIGEONS

It was the form of the thing, the unmanaged
symmetry of it, of whatever it was
he convoked as he knelt on the sidewalk
and laid out from his unfastened briefcase
a benefaction of breadcrumbs—this band

arriving of the unhoused and opportune
we have always with us, composing
as they fed, heads together, wing tip
and tail edge serrated like chicory
(that heavenly weed, that cerulean

commoner of waste places), but with a
glimmer in it, as though the winged
beings of all the mosaics of Ravenna
had gotten the message somehow and come
flying in to rejoin the living: plump-

contoured as the pomegranates and pears
in a Della Robbia holiday wreath that had
put on the bloom, once again, of the soon
to perish, to begin to decay, to re-enter
that dance of freewheeling dervishes,

the breakdown of order: it was the form
of the thing, if a thing is what it was,
and not the merest wisp of a part of
a process—this unraveling inkling
of the envisioned, of states of being

past alteration, of all that we've
never quite imagined except by way of
the body: the winged proclamations,
the wheelings, the stairways, the
vast, concentric, paradisal rose.

TIDEWATER WINTER

After the treetop-filtered
tangerine of dawn,
the zenith's frescoed-by-
Tiepolo cerulean,

an afterglow of thinnest
autumn-crocus-tinted
porcelain, looked up into
through seedpod-

skeletal crape myrtles:
the light for days
replayed itself in some such
phased transparencies,

then dimmed one morning
to a daylong monochrome
of snow, and on the next to
ground fog's numb,

windless whiteness,
muting the waterways,
muffling the cypresses'
pendulous residues

of other weathers, the
dried chandeliers
of tulip trees, the sweet gums'
dangled pomanders,

muffling the lumberyards,
pine plantations, warehouses,
the hunched or gangling
shapes of enterprises

either with or without
proclaiming patronyms
(here's Nabisco, here's Lone Star
Cement); the loading platforms,

watertanks and power lines. Along
the borders of the cypress-knee-
filled, thawed or frozen
inlets of the Chickahominy,

the locomotive sways and sings
the long single
song, the brayed, incessant,
searching syllable

of passing through, of
always moving on.
Tidewater left behind, by Richmond
the ground fog's gone.

THE WATERFALL

Orb-weaver shivering
among the filaments: how many
fibers generated from within
transect the air?

How many hirsute, sightless
gropings anchor
these redwood trees, suffuse
the flowery traceries

of the oxalis? The veining
in this hand, these
eyeballs, the circuitous
and scintillating

leap within the brain—
the synapse,
the waterfall, the black-
thread mane of fern

beside it—all, all
suspend, here:
everywhere, existences
hang by a hair

A HERMIT THRUSH

Nothing's certain. Crossing, on this longest day,
the low-tide-uncovered isthmus, scrambling up
the scree-slope of what at high tide
will be again an island,

to where, a decade since well-being staked
the slender, unpremeditated claim that brings us
back, year after year, lugging the
makings of another picnic—

the cucumber sandwiches, the sea-air-sanctified
fig newtons—there's no knowing what the slamming
seas, the gales of yet another winter
may have done. Still there,

the gust-beleaguered single spruce tree,
the ant-thronged, root-snelled moss, grass
and clover tuffet underneath it,
edges frazzled raw

but, like our own prolonged attachment, holding.
Whatever moral lesson might commend itself,
there's no use drawing one,
there's nothing here

to seize on as exemplifying any so-called virtue
(holding on despite adversity, perhaps) or
any no-more-than-human tendency—
stubborn adherence, say,

to a wholly wrongheaded tenet. Though to
hold on in any case means taking less and less
for granted, some few things seem nearly
certain, as that the longest day

will come again, will seem to hold its breath,
the months-long exhalation of diminishment
again begin. Last night you woke me
for a look at Jupiter,

that vast cinder wheeled unblinking
in a bath of galaxies. Watching, we traveled
toward an apprehension all but impossible
to be held onto—

that no point is fixed, that there's no foothold
but roams untethered save by such snells,
such sailor's knots, such stays
and guy wires as are

mainly of our own devising. From such an
empyrean, aloof seraphic mentors urge us
to look down on all attachment,
on any bonding, as

in the end untenable. Base as it is, from
year to year the earth's sore surface
mends and rebinds itself, however
and as best it can, with

thread of cinquefoil, tendril of the magenta
beach pea, trammel of bramble; with easings,
mulchings, fragrances, the gray-green
bayberry's cool poultice—

and what can't finally be mended, the salt air
proceeds to buff and rarefy: the lopped carnage
of the seaward spruce clump weathers
lustrous, to wood-silver.

Little is certain, other than the tide that
circumscribes us, that still sets its term
to every picnic—today we stayed too long
again, and got our feet wet—

and all attachment may prove at best, perhaps,
a broken, a much-mended thing. Watching
the longest day take cover under
a monk's-cowl overcast,

with thunder, rain and wind, then waiting,
we drop everything to listen as a
hermit thrush distills its fragmentary,
hesitant, in the end

unbroken music. From what source (beyond us, or
the wells within?) such links perceived arrive—
diminished sequences so uninsistingly
not even human—there's

hardly a vocabulary left to wonder, uncertain
as we are of so much in this existence, this
botched, cumbersome, much-mended,
not unsatisfactory thing.

from WESTWARD

(1990)

MEADOWLARK COUNTRY

For Doris Thompson Myers

Speaking of the skylark in a New England classroom—
nonbird, upward-twirler, Old-World hyperbole—
I thought how the likewise ground-nesting
Western meadowlark, rather than soar unsupported
out over the cattle range at daybreak, takes up
its post on a fencepost. I heard them out there,
once, by the hundreds, one after another:
a liquid millennium arising from the still
eastward-looking venue of the dark—

like the still-evolving venue of the young, the faces
eastward-looking, bright with a mute,
estranged, ancestral puzzlement.

Ground fog blurring the dogwood,
black haw, sweet gum, sassafras
and hickory along the waterways,
the branches overhead so full
of warblers on the move toward
destinations, habitats they're

ignorant of any need to find
their way to, to explore,
exploit, alter the face of:
prevailing winds, disheveled
shores, the wet brink's tidal
waverings: the branches overhead

so full of small, unfrightened
quicknesses that if you shook
them they'd simply flutter free
in loosened gusts, ink-straked,
eye-ringed, wing-barred, marked
or cowled with dark, or vivid as

these loosening streams—oxblood,
crimson, flame, clear yellow—
from the already stripped, half
stark, half still gorgeous wood-
lands we glimpse in passing.
Glooming through fog, the cypress,

up to its knees in tidal muck,
will likewise stand bare under
the winter rains. The burnished
tenacity of holly and magnolia, the
scissored undercroft of boxwood,
look like permanence. Ringingly,

the mockingbird—a virtuoso in
and out of season—declares
it lives here, unsubjected
to prevailing winds or tides, to
anything it chooses not to notice:
laws, controls, confederations

don't faze its self-assertive
stances: not the stocks, the
statehouse with the Union Jack atop
it, church every Sunday, monuments,
earthworks, battlefields, the vague
repositories of the dead. Upwards

of forty different tribes . . . having
never submitted themselves to any
laws, any coercive power. . . . Were it
made a question, whether no law
or too much law . . . submits man
to the greatest evil, one who

has seen both conditions of
existence would pronounce it
(thus Jefferson) to be the last.
The mockingbird, an opportunist
ready to expand its range where
there's an opening, lives well,

sings in all weathers, gives no
heed to the accustomary collection
of bones, and deposition of them,
in barrows (since obliterated)
by parties moving through the
country, whose expressions were

construed to be those of sorrow:
ignorant of royal grants, crests,
charters, sea power, mercantile
expansion, the imperative to
find an opening, explore, exploit,
and in so doing begin to alter,

with its straking smudge and smear,
little by little, this opening in
the foliage, wet brink of all our
enterprise: the blur of bays, the
estuarial fog at sunrise, the glooms
and glimmerings, the tidal waters.

KUDZU DORMANT

Ropes, pulleys, shawls,
caparisons, tent curtains
the hue of mildew, strung
above the raw, red-gulleyed
wintering hide of Dixie—

rambunctious eyesore,
entrepreneur (as most are)
from away off somewhere,
like the overdressed though
feral daffodils that prosper

under burnt-out chimneys, in
middens, lethargies, debris
of enterprise that's slipped
into the lap of yet another
annal of the poor: deplore

it dormant or, on principle,
admire it green, a panacea
rampant is what's muscled
in—a charming strangler
setting the usual example.

DALLAS—FORT WORTH:
REDBUD AND MISTLETOE

Terrain that from above, aboard the hurled
steel spore, appears suffused with vivid
ravelings, the highways' mimic of veinings

underground, the fossil murk we're all
propelled by, for whatever term: as with
magenta freshets of Texas redbud, curled

among dun oaks fed on by yellowing nuggets
of old mistletoe, the sometime passport
to sulphurous Avernus *(the golden leafage*

rustling in light wind), though here we hugely
deafen to the hiss of Nemesis: *so turns*
the wheel of change; so turns the world.

DELETED PASSAGE

In the dead of January, while snow fell
dwindling, a lisp inside a drafty flue,
lying in bed alone I dreamed of furnaces.
At the bland beginning there were conferees
in a hired room, the scrape of folding chairs,
a chartered bus, and then a border crossed,
a meadow in another climate: deep
in that alien grass, I turned and saw
and recognized at once—changed, strange,
unrecognizable—a friend long dead,
instantaneity of dreaming fusing
fluidity and rigor, the once child-hater
become a shepherdess of children—nymphets
with madonna faces, their long hair flowing
as they ran, as they came racing
through the foreign grass
to offer us, with all the pampered charm
of their estate, the keys: we sat with them
in kitchens and at secret tables,
knowing ourselves beguiled.
                                    And then a change.
There is something I have forgotten: how or why
we are once more on the move, and who is at the wheel
here in the dark, the thrilling foreign dark.
But what, having veered from the ordinary way,
we are seeing, what we are being shown,
is privileged: there is someone
who does not and who must not know
we have been witnesses of what we are now
witness to: dome after dome
along the secret road, enceinte
with scarlet, licking maws.
                                    It is too late.
I have looked, I have seen
the stokers hunkering. It is too late
now to unthink the worst.

SEDER NIGHT

When he lost his way in the Hagodah
　　　they knew: a year from then
the moonlight traveling the bedclothes
　　　would find him gone.

Rooftop-occluded, the Passover moonrise
　　　shrinks to a talisman;
memory's thumbed-over congeries,
　　　year by year, wears down,

goes bald, loses its smell, its senses
　　　to the denomination of a coin,
a pair of cufflinks in a drawer,
　　　a wedding photograph, a son—

an only son, an offshoot of the larger
　　　process of uprooting
from the shtetl, the movement westward—
　　　the ritual yearning:

Jerusalem: assimilations, dispersals,
　　　furnaces: Never again!
The vacated bedclothes, the rising of
　　　the seasonal moon.

IOLA, KANSAS

Riding all night, the bus half empty, toward the interior,
among refineries, trellised and turreted illusory cities,
the crass, the indispensable wastefulness of oil rigs
offshore, of homunculi swigging at the gut of a continent:

the trailers, the semis, the vans, the bumper stickers,
slogans in day-glo invoking the name of Jesus, who knows
what it means: the air waves, the brand name, the backyard
Barbie-doll barbecue, graffiti in video, the burblings,

the dirges: *heart like a rock, I said Kathy I'm lost,*
the scheme is a mess, we've left Oklahoma, its cattle,
sere groves of pecan trees interspersing the horizonless
belch and glare, the alluvium of the auto junkyards,

we're in Kansas now, we've turned off the freeway,
we're meandering, as again night falls, among farmsteads,
the little towns with the name of a girl on the watertower,
the bandstand in the park at the center, the churches

alight from within, perpendicular banalities of glass
candy-streaked purple-green-yellow (who is this Jesus?),
the strangeness of all there is, whatever it is, growing
stranger, we've come to a rest stop, the name of the girl

on the watertower is Iola: no video, no vending machines,
but Wonder Bread sandwiches, a pie: "It's boysenberry,
I just baked it today," the woman behind the counter
believably says, the innards a purply glue, and I eat it

with something akin to reverence: free refills from
the Silex on the hot plate, then back to our seats,
the loud suction of air brakes like a thing alive, and
the voices, the sleeping assembly raised, as by an agency

out of the mystery of the interior, to a community—
and through some duct in the rock I feel my heart go out,
out here in the middle of nowhere (the scheme is a mess)
to the waste, to the not knowing who or why, and am happy.

HAVING LUNCH AT BRASENOSE

Possible by now, one would suppose,
to look out, coming down from London,
at the wheatfield poppies, the dogrose
    and elder, the water meadows,

and after the foursquare nightmare
of cooling towers at Didcot, again
at the occluded, sliding signature
    of domes, finials and spires,

with no particular pang or tremor
for what one had been—irretrievably,
it seemed then to a dazed latecomer—
    so long ago undone by:

the burgeoning of stone, the shiver
everywhere—it was spring, with the
English chill, and one was very young—
    of the longstanding:

sequesterer of such carelessness,
such poise, lit up by the dazzling
gaze of him with whom one was, of
    course, at once in love

overwhelmingly, cravenly half aware
even then it was no merely erotic
trap one had fallen into, it was
    centuries of enclosure,

it was the walls, not the riotous
break-in of all that was happening,
mainly, in one's own imagination:
    the fact of brass,

the shapeliness, the perpendicular
heft of the Bodleian, the Radcliffe Camera's
hovering poise, yes, and the hard nose
    of the eponymous

brazen lion one has now the luck
of another look at, decades later—
to uncover, lodged in a bedrock
    older than marble or

the bronze of monuments, this
brazen waif, this changeling—
the intransigeance, the airy
    indignity of being young.

WESTWARD

For Anthony Kemp

Distance is dead. At Gatwick, at Heathrow
the loud spoor, the grinding tremor,
manglings, accelerated trade routes

in reverse: the flyblown exotic place,
the heathen shrine exposed. A generation
saw it happen: the big-eyed, spindling

overleapers of the old slow silk route
shiver in terylene at Euston, grimed
caravansary of dispersal, where a lone

pigeon circles underneath the girders,
trapped in the breaking blur of sound waves—
a woman's sourceless voice interminably

counting off the terminals, a sibyl's
lapful of uncertainties. There's trouble
to the north, the trains are late: from

knotted queues the latest émigrés
of a spent Commonwealth look up: so many,
drawn toward what prospect, from what

point of origin? Bound for Iona in
the Western Isles, doleful, unlulled
by British Rail, lying awake I listen

to the clicking metronome as time
runs out, feeling the old assumptions,
aired, worm-tunneled, crumble,

thinking of the collapse of distance:
Proust's paradise of the unvisited,
of fool's-gold El Dorado. At Glasgow

there's still trouble, but the train
to Oban's running. Rain seeps in;
past the streaked, streaming pane,

a fir-fringed, sodden glimpse, the
verberation of a name: Loch Lomond.
"Really?" The callow traveler opposite

looks up, goes back to reading—yes,
it really is Thucydides: hubris,
brazen entitlements, forepangs of

letting go, all that. At Oban, a wet
trek to the ferry landing, where a
nun, or the daft counterfeit of one

(time runs out, the meek grow jaded,
shibboleths of piety no guarantee):
veil and wimple above dank waterproof,

nun-blue pantsuit protruding—lugs
half a dozen satchels ("tinned things
you can't get up here"), has misplaced

her ticket, is so fecklessly egregious
it can't (or could it, after all?) be
contraband. From Craignure, Isle of Mull,

a bus jolts westward, traversing, and
it's still no picnic, the slow route
Keats slogged through on that wet

walking tour: a backward-looking
homage, not a setting forth, as for
his brother George, into the future:

drowned Lycidas, whether beyond the
stormy . . . And of course it rained,
the way it's doing as I skitter up

the cleated iron of the gangway at
Fionnphort; Iona, an indecipherable
blur, a slosh of boots and oilskins,

once landed on, is even wetter.
Not that it always rains: tomorrow
everything will be diaphanous

as the penumbra of a jellyfish:
I'll ride to Staffa over tourmaline
and amethyst without a wrinkle;

will stand sun-warmed above the bay
where St. Columba made his pious landfall,
the purple, ankle-deep, hung like a mantle

on the starved shoulder of the moor.
Heather! I'd thought, the year I first
set foot, in Maine, among blueberries'

belled, pallid scurf; then—But there's
no heather *here*. Right to begin with:
botanically, they're all one family.

I saw that pallor, then, as an attenuation
in the west: the pioneers, the children's
children of the pioneers, look up from

the interior's plowed-under grassland,
the one homeland they know no homeland
but a taken-over turf: no sanction, no cover

but the raveled sleeve of empire: and yearn
for the pristine, the named, the fabulous,
the holy places. But from this island—

its nibbled turf, sheep trails, rabbit
droppings, harebells, mosses' brass-
starred, sodden firmament, the plink

of plover on that looped, perennial,
vast circumnavigation: at ground level
an incessant whimpering as everything,

however minuscule, joins the resistance
to the omnipresent wind—the prospect
is to the west. Here at the raw edge

of Europe—limpet tenacities, the tidal
combings, purplings of kelp and dulse,
the wrack, the blur, the breakup

of every prospect but turmoil, of
upheaval in the west—the retrospect
is once again toward the interior:

backward-looking, child of the child
of pioneers, forward-slogging with
their hooded caravels, their cattle,

and the fierce covered coal of doctrine
from what beleaguered hearth-fire of
the Name, they could not speculate,

such was the rigor of the Decalogue's
Thou Shalt Not—I now discover that
what looked, still looks, like revelation

was not hell-fire, no air-splintering
phosphorus of injunction, no Power,
no force whatever, but an opening

at the water's edge: a little lake,
world's eye, the mind's counterpart,
an eyeblink of reflection wrung from

the unreflecting seethe and chirr and
whimper of the prairie, the wind-
stirred grass, incognizant incognito

(all flesh being grass) of the mind's
resistance to the omnipresence of what
moves but has no, cannot say its name.

There at the brim of an illumination
that can't be entered, can't be lived in—
you'd either founder, a castaway, or drown—

a well, a source that comprehends, that
supersedes all doctrine: what surety,
what reprieve from drowning, is there,

other than in names? The prairie eyeblink,
stirred, grows murmurous—a murderous,
a monstrous world rimmed by the driftwood

of embarkations, landings, dooms, conquests,
missionary journeys, memorials: Columba
in the skin-covered wicker of that coracle,

lofting these stonily decrepit preaching
posts above the heathen purple; in their
chiseled gnarls, dimmed by the weatherings

of a millennium and more, the braided syntax
of a zeal ignited somewhere to the east,
concealed in hovels, quarreled over,

portaged westward: a basket weave, a
fishing net, a weir to catch, to salvage
some tenet, some common intimation for

all flesh, to hold on somehow till
the last millennium: as though the routes,
the ribbonings and redoublings, the

attenuations, spent supply lines, frayed-
out gradual of the retreat from empire, all
its castaways, might still bear witness.

ALDERS

The roadway's sallow, puddled furrow
uncurls like a root among the alders,
then flops up where the granite surfaces,
a bare outcrop. Alders are hard to stop—
impossible, even, unless you're really serious.

Someone who wasn't, from the look
of it, has done a little hacking at them
along the edges; but to deal with the alder—
the way it's dealt with down by the inlet—
means slash and burn, year by year by year.

It's not only the alders. Nothing's
the way it was. The jack pine's closing in
a herd of brassy, burgeoning antlers
now bars the opening down to the shore.
Cut off, branch-stung, I find myself in tears

for all sorts of likely and unlikely reasons.
We try another way, between green-creamy
headlamps of mountain ash, wet peat moss
underfoot, dim elegiac voices of white-
throated sparrows above a dwindling trace

we halfway recognize, to a high ledge
where we once picnicked—a tight, finical
medallion that turns out to be a bench mark
setting its seal on the would-be primeval,
while everywhere the alders take the tundra back,

take back the fields and the four cellar holes
left by the settlers who made it their business,
come spring, to clear away the winter's frost-
heaved boulders, and to keep down the alders.
I'd once supposed these acres had no past—

that entity, no virgin, bled with the season,
burgeoned, withered, bloomed and bled again,
uninterfered with, like the pattern of a dance,
not the unarmed uprising of this
landlock, these tough true inhabitants.

BLUEBERRYING IN AUGUST

Sprung from the hummocks
of this island, stemmed,
sea-spray-fed chromosomes
trait-coded, say, for eyes
of that surprising blue
some have, that you have:
they're everywhere, these
mimic apertures the color
of distances, of drowning—

of creekside bluebells
islanded in the lost world
of childhood; of the
illusory indigo that moats
these hillocks when
the air is windless.

Today, though, there is
wind: a slate sag occludes
the afternoon with old,
hound-throated mutterings.
Offshore, the lighthouse
fades to a sheeted,
sightless ghost. August
grows somber. Though the blue-
eyed chromosome gives way,
living even so, minute to
minute, was never better.

A WHIPPOORWILL IN THE WOODS

Night after night, it was very nearly enough,
they said, to drive you crazy: a whippoorwill
in the woods repeating itself like the stuck groove
of an LP with a defect, and no way possible
        of turning the thing off.

And night after night, they said, in the insomniac
small hours the whipsawing voice of obsession
would have come in closer, the way a sick
thing does when it's done for—or maybe the reason
        was nothing more melodramatic

than a night-flying congregation of moths, lured in
in their turn by house-glow, the strange heat
of it—imagine the nebular dangerousness, if one
were a moth, the dark pockmarked with beaks, the great
        dim shapes, the bright extinction—

if moths are indeed, after all, what a whippoorwill
favors. Who knows? Anyhow, from one point of view
insects are to be seen as an ailment, moths above all:
the filmed-over, innumerable nodes of spun-out tissue
        untidying the trees, the larval

spew of such hairy hordes, one wonders what use
they can be other than as a guarantee no bird
goes hungry. We're like that. The webbiness,
the gregariousness of the many are what we can't abide.
        We single out for notice

above all what's disjunct, the way birds are,
with their unhooked-up, cheekily anarchic
dartings and flashings, their uncalled-for color—
the indelible look of the rose-breasted grosbeak
        an aunt of mine, a noticer

of such things before the noticing had or needed
a name, drew my five-year-old attention up to, in
the green deeps of a maple. She never married,
believed her cat had learned to leave birds alone,
       and for years, node after node,

by lingering degrees she made way within for
what wasn't so much a thing as it was a system,
a webwork of error that throve until it killed her.
What is health? We must all die sometime.
       Whatever it is, out there

in the woods, that begins to seem like
a species of madness, we survive as we can:
the hooked-up, the humdrum, the brief, tragic
wonder of being at all. The whippoorwill out in
       the woods, for me, brought back

as by a relay, from a place at such a distance
no recollection now in place could reach so far,
the memory of a memory she told me of once:
of how her father, my grandfather, by whatever
       now unfathomable happenstance,

carried her (she might have been five) into the breathing night.
"Listen!" she said he'd said. "Did you hear it?
That was a whippoorwill." And she (and I) never forgot.

A WINTER BURIAL

From tall rooms, largesse of peonies,
the porches summercool, the bed upstairs
immaculate in its white counterpane,

to kerosene-lit evenings, the wind
an orphan roaming the silver maples,
sudden widowhood: to meaner comforts,

a trumpetvine above the kitchen door,
then one night her new husband didn't
come in from the milking: to the lot

she bought with what that place went
for, dwindlings in a doll's house: to
the high-rise efficiency condominium,

television on all day, to the cubicle
in the denominational home, to total
unprivacy of bed and bedpan, nurse shoes,

TV with no picture or else coming in waves,
a vertigo: to, one nightfall when the last
weak string gave way that had held whatever

she was, that mystery, together, the bier
that waited—there were no planes coming in,
not many made it to the funeral, the blizzard

had been so bad, the graveyard drifted
so deep, so many severed limbs of trees
thrown down, they couldn't get in to plow

an opening for the hearse, or shovel
the cold white counterpane from that cell
in the hibernal cupboard, till the day after.

SAVANNAH

For Bee Close Lane

Not quite diaphanous, not Spanish,
not a moss, weft after weft
depends from chambered
rafterings of liveoak,
green square leading
to green square, from
opening to opening, as
in a courtship—at whose
discovered center leaps
this rose-leaf
relinquishment,
this falling.
             Yes.
To fall. To ripen
and then wither.
That is all.
                Oh, not all
at all. The bed-curtained,
quickening and ripening
dream of the body,
of fair women, torn
by an obelisk
to the Confederate dead:
the ramparts breached,
the powder magazine's
uproar, the maimed,
sullen giving way,
inform these
mansionings.
             A stillness
out there, past thicketings
of juniper, bullbrier
and yaupon, flailed
thrashings of palmetto,
out past the hiss
of cordgrass:

enveloping
the drop-sleeve
creak of shrimp boats,
a dim, large,
smothering,
incessant
shrug.

AMHERST

May 15, 1987

The oriole, a charred and singing coal,
still burns aloud among the monuments,
its bugle call to singularity the same
unheard (she wrote) as to the crowd,
this graveyard gathering, the audience
           she never had.

Fame has its own dynamic, its smolderings
and ignitions, its necessary distance:
Colonel Higginson, who'd braved the cannon,
admitted his relief not to live near such
breathless, hushed excess (you cannot
           fold a flood,

she wrote, and put it in a drawer), such
stoppered prodigies, compressions and
devastations within the atom—*all this
world contains: his face*—the civil
wars of just one stanza. A universe
           might still applaud,

the red at bases of the trees (she wrote)
like mighty footlights burn, God still
look on, his badge a raised hyperbole—
inspector general of all that carnage,
those gulfs, those fleets and crews
           of solid blood:

the battle fought between the soul and No
One There, no one at all, where cities
ooze away: unbroken prairies of air
without a settlement. On Main Street
the hemlock hedge grows up untrimmed,
           the light that poured

in once like judgment (whether it was noon
at night, or only heaven at noon, she wrote,
she could not tell) cut off, the wistful,
the merely curious, in her hanging dress discern
an ikon; her ambiguities are made a shrine,
              then violated;

we've drunk champagne above her grave, declaimed
the lines of one who dared not live aloud.
I thought of writing her (Dear Emily, though,
seems too intrusive, Dear Miss Dickinson too prim)
to ask, not without irony, what, wherever she
              is now, is made

of all the racket, whether she's of two minds
still; and tell her how on one cleared hillside,
an ample peace that looks toward Norwottuck's
unaltered purple has been shaken since
by bloodshed on Iwo Jima, in Leyte Gulf
              and Belleau Wood.

EASEDALE TARN

Annuities of peat moss,
sedge, bog cotton, bracken
to be trekked through

halfway up the beck's hung
watershed, today still
unwalled common, where

a sheep, though owned
and earmarked, may
still go astray, may

utter its little cry, or,
suddenly aware of where
it's come to—this crag,

this waterfall, this rosebush
arched and glittering
beside it—freeze,

feel the earth's forward
motion, its hurtling,
harrowing retrograde:

past farmsteads, through
gated openings they,
Dorothy and William,

must also, repeatedly,
have passed through,
bound for the source

of all the babble
down there among the
hollies and the hazels—

the mountain basin
still withheld from
view, though to the

inland-moving gulls
that hang above it
it's in no way secret,

nor is it to these
vaporous tributaries,
nor to the air that's

everywhere the habitat
of rising to just such
occasions as the twain

who once inhaled it, in
this very place, may be
said to have invented—

primeval cisterns'
tremor, the blazing
drumskin of rain.

VACANT LOT WITH POKEWEED

Tufts, follicles, grubstake
biennial rosettes, a low-
life beach-blond scruff of
couch grass: notwithstanding
the interglinting dregs

of wholesale upheaval and
dismemberment, weeds do not
hesitate, the wheeling
rise of the ailanthus halts
at nothing—and look! here's

a pokeweed, sprung from seed
dropped by some vagrant, that's
seized a foothold: a magenta-
girdered bower, gazebo twirls
of blossom rounding into

raw-buttoned, garnet-rodded
fruit one more wayfarer
perhaps may salvage from
the season's frittering,
the annual wreckage.

A HEDGE OF RUBBER TREES

The West Village by then was changing; before long
the rundown brownstones at its farthest edge
would have slipped into trendier hands. She lived,
impervious to trends, behind a potted hedge of
rubber trees, with three cats, a canary—refuse
from whose cage kept sifting down and then
germinating, a yearning seedling choir, around
the saucers on the windowsill—and an inexorable
cohort of roaches she was too nearsighted to deal
with, though she knew they were there, and would
speak of them, ruefully, as of an affliction that
     might once, long ago, have been prevented.

Unclassifiable castoffs, misfits, marginal cases:
when you're one yourself, or close to it, there's
a reassurance in proving you haven't quite gone
under by taking up with somebody odder than you are.
Or trying to. "They're my *friends*," she'd say of
her cats—Mollie, Mitzi and Caroline, their names were,
and she was forever taking one or another in a cab
to the vet—as though she had no others. The roommate
who'd become a nun, the one who was Jewish, the couple
she'd met on a foliage tour, one fall, were all people
she no longer saw. She worked for a law firm, said all
     the judges were alcoholic, had never voted.

But would sometimes have me to dinner—breaded veal,
white wine, strawberry Bavarian—and sometimes, from
what she didn't know she was saying, I'd snatch a shred
or two of her threadbare history. Baltic cold. Being
sent home in a troika when her feet went numb. In
summer, carriage rides. A swarm of gypsy children
driven off with whips. An octogenarian father, bishop
of a dying schismatic sect. A very young mother
who didn't want her. A half-brother she met just once.
Cousins in Wisconsin, one of whom phoned her from a candy
store, out of the blue, while she was living in Chicago.
     What had brought her there, or when, remained unclear.

As did much else. We'd met in church. I noticed first
a big, soaring soprano with a wobble in it, then
the thickly wreathed and braided crimp in the mouse-
gold coiffure. Old? Young? She was of no age.
Through rimless lenses she looked out of a child's,
or a doll's, globular blue. Wore Keds the year round,
tended otherwise to overdress. Owned a mandolin. Once
I got her to take it down from the mantel and plink out,
through a warm fuddle of sauterne, a lot of giddy Italian
airs from a songbook whose pages had started to crumble.
The canary fluffed and quivered, and the cats, amazed,
       came out from under the couch and stared.

What could the offspring of schismatic age and a
reluctant child bride expect from life? Not much.
Less and less. A dream she'd had kept coming back,
years after. She'd taken a job in Washington with
some right-wing lobby, and lived in one of those
bow-windowed mansions that turn into roominghouses,
and her room there had a full-length mirror: oval,
with a molding, is the way I picture it. In her dream
something woke her, she got up to look, and there
in the glass she saw she had no face, or whatever
face she'd had was covered over—she gave it
       a wondering emphasis—with gray veils.

The West Village was changing. I was changing. The last
time I asked her to dinner, she didn't show. Hours—
or was it days?—later, she phoned to explain: she hadn't
been able to find my block; a patrolman had steered her home.
I spent my evenings canvassing for Gene McCarthy. Passing,
I'd see her shades drawn, no light behind the rubber trees.
She wasn't out, she didn't own a TV. She was in there,
getting gently blotto. What came next, I wasn't brave
enough to want to know. Only one day, passing, I saw
new shades, quick-chic matchstick bamboo, going up where
the waterstained old ones had been, and where the seedlings—
       O gray veils, gray veils—had risen and gone down.

MY COUSIN MURIEL

From Manhattan, a glittering shambles
of enthrallments and futilities, of leapers
in leotards, scissoring vortices blurred,
this spring evening, by the *punto in aria*
of hybrid pear trees in bloom (no troublesome
fruit to follow) my own eyes are drawn to—
childless spinner of metaphor, in touch
by way of switchboard and satellite, for
the last time ever, with my cousin Muriel:

mother of four, worn down by arthritis,
her kidneys wasting, alone in a hospital
somewhere in California: in that worn voice,
the redhead's sassy timbre eroded from it,
while the unspeakable stirs like a stone,
a strange half-absence and a tone of weakness
(Wordsworth's discharged soldier comes to mind)
as she inquires, fatigued past irony, "How's
your work going?" As for what was hers—

nursing-home steam-table clamor, scummed
soup fat, scrubbed tubers, bones, knives,
viscera, cooking odors lived with till
they live with you, a settlement in the
olfactory tissue—well, it's my function
to imagine scenes, try for connections
as I'm trying now: a grope for words,
the numb, all but immobilized trajectory
to where my cousin, whom I've seen just once

since she went there to live, lies dying:
part of the long-drawn larger movement
that lured the Reverend Charles Wadsworth
to San Francisco, followed in imagination
from the cupola of the shuttered homestead
in Amherst where a childless recluse,
on a spring evening a century ago, A.D.

(so to speak) 1886, would cease to breathe
the air of rural Protestant New England—

an atmosphere and a condition which
by stages, wagon trains, tent meetings,
the Revival, infused the hinterland
my cousin Muriel and I both hailed from:
a farmhouse childhood, kerosene-lit,
tatting-and-mahogany genteel. "You
were the smart one," she'd later say.
Arrant I no doubt was; as for imagining
scenes, it must be she'd forgotten

the melodramas she once improvised above
the dolls' tea-table: "For the pity's sake!
How could you get us all in such a fix?
Well, I s'pose we'll just have to make
the best of it"—the whole trajectory of
being female, while I played the dullard,
presaged. She bloomed, knew how to flirt,
acquired admirers. I didn't. In what I now
recall as a last teen-age heart-to-heart,

I'm saying I don't plan on getting married.
"Not ever?" "Not ever"—then, craven, "Oh,
I'd like to be *engaged*." Which is what she
would have been, by then, to Dorwin Voss,
whom I'd been sweet on in fifth grade (last
painless crush before the crash of puberty)—
blue-eyed, black-haired, good-looking Dorwin,
who'd later walk out on her and their kids,
moving on again, part of the larger exodus

from the evangel-haunted prairie hinterland.
Some stayed; the more intemperate of us
headed east—a Village basement, uptown
lunch hours, vertiginous delusions of

autonomy, the bar crowd; waiting for
some well-heeled dullard of a male to
deign to phone, or for a stumbling-
drunk, two-timing spouse's key to turn
the small-hour dark into another fracas—

others for California: the lettuce fields,
Knott's Berry Farm, the studios; palms,
slums, sprinklers, canyon landslides,
fuchsia hedges hung with hummingbirds,
the condominium's kempt squalor: whatever
Charles Wadsworth, out there, foresaw
as consolation for anyone at all—attached,
estranged, or merely marking time—little
is left, these days, these times, to say

when the unspeakable stirs like a stone.
Pulled threads, the shared fabric of a
summer memory: the state fair campground,
pump water, morning light through tent flaps,
the promenade among the booths: blue-ribbon
zinnias and baby beeves, the cooled marvel
of a cow, life size, carved out of butter;
a gypsy congeries without a shadow on it
but the domed torpor of the capitol

ballooning, ill at ease, egregious
souvenir of pomp among the cornfields;
kewpie-doll lowlife along the midway,
the bleachers after dark where, sick
with mirth, under the wanton stars,
for the ineptitude of clowns, we soared
in arabesques of phosphorus, and saw—
O dread and wonder, O initiating taste
of ecstasy—a man shot from a cannon.

Too young then to know how much we knew
already of experience, how little of
its wider paradigm, enthralled by that
punto in aria of sheer excitement, we who
are neither leaf nor bole—O hybrid
pear tree, cloned fruitless blossomer!—
suspend, uprooted from the hinterland,
this last gray filament across a continent
where the unspeakable stirs like a stone.

NOTHING STAYS PUT

In memory of Father Flye, 1884–1985

The strange and wonderful are too much with us.
The protea of the antipodes—a great,
globed, blazing honeybee of a bloom—
for sale in the supermarket! We are in
our decadence, we are not entitled.
What have we done to deserve
all the produce of the tropics—
this fiery trove, the largesse of it
heaped up like cannonballs, these pineapples, bossed
and crested, standing like troops at attention,
these tiers, these balconies of green, festoons
grown sumptuous with stoop labor?

The exotic is everywhere, it comes to us
before there is a yen or a need for it. The green-
grocers, uptown and down, are from South Korea.
Orchids, opulence by the pailful, just slightly
fatigued by the plane trip from Hawaii, are
disposed on the sidewalks; alstroemerias, freesias
fattened a bit in translation from overseas; gladioli
likewise estranged from their piercing ancestral crimson;
as well as, less altered from the original blue cornflower
of the roadsides and railway embankments of Europe, these
bachelor's buttons. But it isn't the railway embankments
their featherweight wheels of cobalt remind me of, it's

a row of them among prim colonnades of cosmos,
snapdragon, nasturtium, bloodsilk red poppies,
in my grandmother's garden: a prairie childhood,
the grassland shorn, overlaid with a grid,
unsealed, furrowed, harrowed and sown with immigrant grasses,
their massive corduroy, their wavering feltings embroidered
here and there by the scarlet shoulder patch of cannas
on a courthouse lawn, by a love knot, a cross stitch
of living matter, sown and tended by women,
nurturers everywhere of the strange and wonderful,
beneath whose hands what had been alien begins,
as it alters, to grow as though it were indigenous.

But at this remove what I think of as
strange and wonderful, strolling the side streets of Manhattan
on an April afternoon, seeing hybrid pear trees in blossom,
a tossing, vertiginous colonnade of foam, up above—
is the white petalfall, the warm snowdrift
of the indigenous wild plum of my childhood.
Nothing stays put. The world is a wheel.
All that we know, that we're
made of, is motion.

THE PRAIRIE

. . . her praises celebrated by no one, she is needed by no one,
and amid her joyous accents you detect the melancholy call for
"A bard! a bard!"

ANTON CHEKHOV, "The Steppe"

. . . that everything in this life is, in a sense, but a pattern in a
carpet. Trodden underfoot.

JOSEPH BRODSKY, "Flying from Byzantium"

1

The wind whines in the elevator shaft. The houseless
squinny at us, mumbling. We walk attuned
to the colubrine rustle of a proletariat

that owes nobody anything, through a Manhattan
otherwise (George Eliot's phrase) well wadded
with stupidity—a warren of unruth, a propped

vacuity: our every pittance under lock and key
a party to the general malfeasance. Saurian,
steam-wreathed rancors crowd the manholes,

as though somebody grappled with the city's
entrails: Laocoön, doomsayer, by a god
or gods undone. Whom nobody believed, of course.

No, better, as the muse of what's become
of us, invoke Chekhov's imagined Jew who put—
out of demented principle—the rubles he'd

inherited into the stove. Money-burning:
however jaded you may think you are, now there's
a scandal for you. Six thousand rubles,

and he burns them: shows no respect, fears
no one, is a man possessed, the evil sprite
out of a nightmare: thus Chekhov, scandal-

mongering. Grandson of a serf, son of a
storekeeper, brought up to the chink of kopecks
at Taganrog: spring mud and summer dust,

burdocks, beatings, piety. Money and profits:
the mainspring for all of us, except that brother
of a tavernkeeping Jew, who mocks us,

boasting he put his money in the stove.
So Chekhov tells us—who, half a nomad,
consorted with the nomads of Sakhalin—yurt-

dwellers who never washed, who planted nothing,
saw the plow as a transgression; whose numbers
were already in decline; who smelled, up close,

as all unbathed and houseless wanderers do,
of sweat, soil, urine: living nit-encrusted,
matted, shivering. One forgets, here in

half-stupefied Manhattan, how much of everything
that happens happens (Simone Weil's relentless
phrase) far from hot baths. The wind howls

from across the Hudson: lost, lost. Marx
and Engels, Lenin, Red October: since Chekhov
(no ideologue) wrote of the general malfeasance

"We do not care, it does not interest us,"
however much has changed, still nothing changes.
Demagoguery. Boundaries. Forced marches.

Monoculture on the heels of slash and burn.
Land reform. Drought. Insects. Drainage.
Long-term notes. Collectives. Tractor lugs.

Names: brunizem and chernozem; culm,
rhizome and stolon. A fibrous, root-fattened
hinterland of grass. The steppe. The prairie.

A chance fact leaps into place: that Anton Chekhov
came howling (as only the stillborn can
fail to do) into existence at Taganrog

the year my father's father, no doubt howling
too, endured the shock of entry. Add the link
of early memory: the prairie, the steppe—

a shimmering caul of namelessness, of voices,
unauthenticated, multitudinous, in wait
for (so Chekhov wrote) a muse, a scribe, a bard.

2

The year is 1860. February. Still hard winter.
A cabin of hewn logs, on sixty acres
of raw grassland, prairie yet unturned.

One bed. Snow sifts through roof chinks.
Some nights the kettle freezes on the stove.
My great-grandfather gets what rest he can

on a quilt-covered pile of straw. A settler
from Indiana, his mind scarred by whippings;
a smattering of schooling, an appetite for land.

A hinterland of grass: tough, fertile,
root-nurtured chernozem ("black earth"
in Russian), nameless hitherto: lush midriff

of an empire Napoleon, having retaken it
from Spain (who didn't exactly own it) was now
hard pressed to trade for cash: bought in a hurry,

unlooked-at, for four cents an acre, by envoys
who'd exceeded their instructions, but who knew
what was imperative: land so rich, the more-

than-man-high panicles so dense, the nomad
aborigines for centuries had shunned it. Treaties
and forced marches brought them to it—treaties

made by chiefs who knew no better. Boundaries
were drawn; section by quarter section
platted, parceled, sold, speculated on,

built on; torn open, for the first time ever,
by plowshares—shouldering a dimming memory
of what had been, would never be again, aside.

A dimming memory of campsites: skin cones
smoke-stained, the base aglow, the moving shadow
of the life within revealed: two half circles

ranged about the sacred tree-bole, gift of
Wakonda, shining summoner of thunderbirds from
their imagined corners. A dimming memory of how,

toward the ending of the Moon When Nothing Happens,
spring thunder and the early-morning trilling
of meadowlarks returned, among the sloughs

the whooping cranes moved in again to dance
before they coupled—carmine-faced up close,
like painted women—and on higher ground

big-wattled prairie chickens thudded, courting.
All long gone. My father's father, as a boy
prone to anxieties, night terrors, straying

sometimes at dusk in unfenced spaces where
bell-clappered cattle roamed, had seen them—grand,
pagan, dreadful as the tree-bole of Ashtoreth.

The white man does not understand America,
a red man wrote: *the roots of the tree of his life
have yet to grasp it.* A dwindling memory

among the Omaha, a woodland people once,
whose remnant, up close, smell of the usual
sweat, soil, urine, vomit: a way of living lost.

Hard work. The settlers put a beleaguered foot down
against the shiftless, as their forebears had
concerning maypoles and the sanctus bell. Hard

work. Drainage ditches. Fences to keep in
the cattle. Now and then a grown man, entoiled
by evangelical dismay, would cry, "Lost! Lost!"

3

A nerve storm, a lapse or lesion, a blizzard
in the brain: at sixteen, grown up bookish,
hesitant, susceptible, my father's father

would blurt—his little sister looking up aghast,
the half-cleared supper table a bleak witness—
something about being done for, damned to hell—

something like that; to find, almost before his mother,
always the quicker one, could speak, the revulsion
gone; elation following, an astonished lightness.

What did it mean? He was never sure. A brimstone
rhetoric imbibed? A flareup—something in the glands,
like acne? He'd put it, at all events, behind him.

At twenty, wary of certitude, he shared questions,
and a bed, with one best friend. Nights, they
read Emerson together; after the swimming wick

went under, they'd go on talking. What was it
kept him so often wakeful, awed, while
the friend slept—what plank in reason, laid

unbroken, precarious, across the slough
of namelessness, its chucklings, its slitherings,
its shrieks, its spearheaded leaps and lunges?

Egorooshka, Chekhov's child-deputy, cocooned
among the wool bales, crossing the steppe,
heard the uneasy buzz and stir, the turmoil

when the wind rose. *An inlet into the deeps
of Reason*, Emerson had written: *out of
unhandseled savage nature, out of the terrible*

*Druids and Berserkirs . . . We have listened too long
to the courtly muses. In self-trust all the virtues
are comprehended. . . .* Self-trust. Man Thinking.

When—my father's father might have wondered—
was Man Thinking, self-reliant, other than
alone in the vast stammer of the inarticulate?

An absence. Creeks and timber. Wild plum, crabapple,
sumac along the fencerows. Tilled acres. Section lines.
Farmsteads that clot the vacancy, that cannot fill it—

the sense of exile, of something wrong: a dim
compunction finds Man Thinking anxious, as
all animals are anxious. In heath, duneland,

savanna, all treeless spaces, the immersing
sense of waiting, the unfathomable lassitude,
the purling, the quick tenuity of things.

The dead, wrote Emerson, aged twenty-two, *sleep*
in their moonless night. All history is an epitaph.
A few days more, and idle eyes will run

over your obituary, the world forget you.
The tenuity of being: Chekhov, who'd later
become a doctor, down with a fever, crossing

the steppe, tended by that innkeeping Jew.
My father's father ill with typhoid in a
Dakota roominghouse, a jolting two-day train ride

away from home. In that region of wind he'd bought,
with borrowed money, a treeless piece of land.
Back here, he'd met a girl—small, sprightly, husky-

voiced—who promised, when he headed north again,
to write. He found the homesteaders burning hay
for fuel. The season was wet and cold, the wind unending.

By midsummer he'd turned, with team and plow,
the sod of eighty hitherto uncultivated acres.
He took his bride there on their honeymoon.

      4

We have listened too long to the courtly muses.
Perhaps. My father's father, from the spring
he turned the sod out there, preserved a sonnet:

There crowd my mind (he wrote) *vague fancies*
of Aeolian harpings, twined with weird oaks'
murmurings. In those wind-scathed solitudes,

impelled by absence so immense it all but
unpropped Man Thinking, he'd reached for that
old lore for reassurance—as one day a grandchild,

likewise impelled, would travel eastward,
backward to the precincts of grass-overrun,
mere, actual Dodona. A venture he'd

have been bemused by. I feel a halfway need
to justify, to whisper, Please don't disapprove,
don't think me frivolous. Can the courtly muses

of Europe, those bedizened crones, survive
the manholes, the vaunt and skitter of Manhattan, or
consort with the dug-in, the hunkering guardians

of the Dakotas? The Louisiana Purchase
passing (as it were) from hand to hand,
my father's father, having staked a claim

by planting trees there, rented out the eighty,
trekked back with his bride, a homing pair,
to set up as a storekeeper's son-in-law.

The year is 1885. Next spring will see a son
delivered yelling into the rooms above the store.
Still nobody is settled. The railroad

has made people restless. Chekhov too: in 1887,
bound from Moscow to Taganrog, he'd cross
the steppe again, this time by rail; would see

the wheelbarrows, the dugouts where the work crews
lived, mounded under the moon. By spring
of that same year, a railborne exodus

to California, the latest Land of Promise,
of figs and pomegranates, had begun. Whole
neighborhoods were going. In September

my grandparents-to-be would be among them.
From an uncushioned sleeping car, the first
arid glimpse of Colorado. The Spanish Peaks.

A washout in New Mexico. Immoderate heat
and chill. The desert's rigors and mirages.
Then Pasadena. Date palms. Dust. Ramshackle

houses. Gamblers. The bare arroyo. The mountain
wall. Pregnant again, my father's mother
had been trainsick all the way. Pasadena:

the name a borrowing from the Chippewa, who'd
never lived there. Of those who did, what history
there is is an erasure. Called—after the mission

that came to save them, that brought in measles
and the common cold—the Gabrielinos, they sickened
as the mission prospered, came to own the valley,

carved it up and sold it off, rancho by rancho.
Irrigated, planted to vines, walnuts, oranges,
with prairie-dwellers hurrying in, the ranchos

yet again were subdivided and sold off: a pandemic
frenzy of land changing hands. *The country's mind,
aimed low, grows thick and fat:* thus Emerson,

who looked for such as ravished from the East to rise,
to blaze forth in the West. A West that proved—as
one, musing, would later write—to be, essentially . . .

5

Essentially a customer: thus the exile, musing
of empire's westward course, of intertwinings:
everything is, in a sense (he wrote), *a pattern*

in a carpet. Trodden underfoot. The West
(in short) *was offering nothing.* Whatever
it might choose to take, it took: zeal, doctrine,

manpower: all trodden underfoot. No new thing
usage cannot foul. Who was San Gabriel? Who
thinks of archangels, of angels in Los Angeles?

That winter, while blizzards caromed screaming
over Dakota, Chekhov in Moscow, out of who knows
what stored-up fervor and revulsion, for

the money-fond, obliging Jew who'd tended him,
brought forth a disturbed, disturbing, money-
loathing brother, with his strange smile, so

complex, expressive of such feeling, in which
what predominated was an unfeigned scorn.
February, the tale written and sent off, would see

my father's father with a surveyor's transit,
plotting a tract of greasewood and sagebrush—
desert really. The wells there would soon go dry.

The year is 1888; the place, North Raymond Avenue
in Pasadena. Here, where many still lived under
canvas, in a shake-roofed, newsprint-papered

shack, long since demolished, on the sixth of April—
no doubt yelling as we've all done—my father
entered on a scene of which he'd have no memory.

They'd stay, all told, not quite two years.
How can a descendant, pondering this, not
pause, bemused by the fortuity of things?

The fever runs its course. Less land
changes hands; more wells fail. Jobs dry up.
Hired by a grocer, for six months my father's

father handled accounts, while sick headaches
made his life hell. Eyestrain, he surmised
it was. What was he good for but what

he'd been brought up as, a dirt farmer?
Unless you counted such a thing as friendship.
The best friend, best he'd ever have, would

stay on out there; would, unracked by misgivings,
prosper. The in-laws would likewise trade,
seduced, a banshee-ridden interior winter

for living at the edge, with earthquakes.
Living at the edge, or near it, the Pacific
twenty miles away: in all that time they'd

never seen it. Driving, one day, a hired team
to Long Beach, where the descendants of ten
thousand settlers these days throng, they found

a boardwalk, a cliff above the moiling surf,
the sands. What did it mean, that roaring?
Existences, as they listen and then turn away,

tremble: fate, memory, seaweed-clotted
poluphloisboio thalassēs pouring in immense,
immersing all and every road not taken:

the pagan muse, unwizened, living out there
at the edge, with earthquakes, not to be
counted on. They listen, turn away, head east

toward an interior without a rim, an absence
that can, and does, unsettle—my father's
mother motion-sick, again, much of the way.

     6

Years later, even so, they'd go again: the journey
through snowdrifts ending in a blaze of oranges,
the bridged arroyo in winter spate, the in-laws

waiting. With the best friend, said now to be
all business, no time for folks, proving how
a mover and shaker could still remember, talk

deep into the night, as always; passing mention
of unease, something the matter with a kidney;
a last wave from the platform. He'd be dead

within a year. Decades after, my father's father
would ponder that luminous implicit thing,
that bonding. Of how it was, what happened,

the language he groped for is all that's left.
The language, the occasional rhyme and meter:
There crowd my mind . . . His letters, her replies,

that spring he'd turned the sod, off in Dakota,
would one day, as so much foolishness, go
up in smoke. Love letters, another medium

of exchange, burned like the rubles. Chekhov
in 1890 trekked eastward, toward the squalors
of Sakhalin; far from hot baths, item by nit-

encrusted, shivering item, he'd spell out
the exiles' situation. My father's father,
meanwhile, spelled out his own: the eighty

they now lived on, the Dakota tree claim, debts
totaling eight hundred; a wife, two boys, a new-
born daughter. The headaches miserably persisted.

Chekhov would come back spitting blood, with
fourteen years to live. My father's father,
prospering, would acquire more land; eventually

he'd own half a section, put up a house, surround
it with shade trees, an orchard. (My earliest memories
are of that place—an eden of wonder, as though

its secret coves had always been.) He'd be named
county surveyor: chain and compass, plumb bob,
witness trees; lost corners, cemeteries,

culverts, highways. The Louisiana Purchase
pieced and platted, all of it owned. Land-
ownership: the sense of it: he found he liked it.

The headaches did not abate. Behind
the gradual increment of ease, a lurking
hint of something wrong. A twitching

about the neck: What? What? Something was wrong.
A tic, a turning or nodding, an assent or
a denial. As a child, trapped in the doldrums

of Sunday morning, an exile from the modern times
I fervently believed in, I'd observe among
the old ones, the settlers and their shriveling

wives, how many were likewise afflicted.
What did it mean? A giving in to what
could not but be? A judgment? Unwilled

adherence to the devil's party? A sclerosis,
he was told, a hardening about the brain stem.
Mortality stared from within. No, he was told:

the tic was functional, a thing that could
be lived with. He did, for forty years.
Lived anxious, as all animals are anxious:

The stasis between fight and flight. The burrow.
The interminable trilling. Unthinkable,
unthinking space. The distances. The stars.

7

The mysteries of what lived out there, the hunter
and the hunted intertwined; the species that
persisted and that vanished, trodden underfoot:

the linked, perishable, humming webs that only
an unformulating mind could follow, trodden
under: the pattern in the carpet, arabesques

of namelessness, of dreamings; the overlaid
procedure, forethought, accumulation. Assets.
Title deeds. Hot baths. Across the globe,

the neat and fearful grid of settlement. What
stays outside dismissed. Consider the puccoon,
the pasqueflower, the compass plant, the vervain,

as no quasi-monoculture will. Consider the
trout lily, the bluebell and bloodroot my father's
mother brought in from the creekside. A domesticator

born, she made her flowerbeds, her houseplants,
her quilt blocks, her tidy, sunny house the norm:
diffident, adorable, quick to throw up her hands at

what didn't match: "Oh, for the land's sake!"
(What in the world, one wonders now, did that mean?)—
wary of phrases, her love letters expendable:

confront her with what won't come in, won't accept
the settlement: the strange smile of the Jew who
burned the rubles: what then? Imagination

turns, still irresponsible, to Henry James,
a landless, exquisite sort of nomad, who found
no comfort for the dolors of Man Thinking

but in hesitations, velleities, the secret coves
of a surprise the landed, pacing their stiff saraband,
could not have known they harbored: a region

unauthenticated hitherto, awaiting, as
the steppe still did, a muse, a scribe, a bard.
Oh, one can guess what he'd have made of

that strange smile: had he not deemed
Oscar Wilde—who'd die shunned, a rococo
affront to landed propriety—unspeakable?

Chekhov (who wrote plays—that's one connection)
also would die abroad: four years after wild
Oscar; six months after *The Cherry Orchard* opened.

Everything connects, you see: the pattern
in the carpet, trodden underfoot, of Property:
Lopakhin out there hacking at treetrunks:

"Mine! The cherry orchard's mine!" He'd
subdivide it, put up cottages where his fore-
bears, serfs, had felt the knout, where he'd gone

barefoot in winter. . . . No slaves on the prairie, it
may be said. Quite true. A war my great-grandfather
served in saw to that. No chattel slavery—

merely treaties and forced marches. Better the rifle,
some would conclude. Black Hawk's War, the massacre
at Spirit Lake. The losers, what's left of them,

nowadays live on the reservation. That's
what it's called, except by those who live there.
French traders, ransacking their hunting grounds,

called them, from their totem, Renard. They knew
themselves as the Mesquakie. Shunted west to Kansas,
sick, bemused by the black riverbottom land

they'd left, cannily they aped the white man's
game, raised cash, made their bid; signed
papers; moved in; took up the settled life.

　　　8

The settled life: no landed estates, no manors,
no eminences grander than the county courthouse
with its spiked cannon, its humdrum pigeonholes.

Woodlots knot the horizon, pull one in.
The gossip. The scathing whisper. Party lines.
Consensus. Stratifyings: oh yes, even in

a place so nearly level, someone to look
down on—renters; hired men and their unwashed
progeny; the drifter from nowhere; the sinner

found out out of wedlock. Fear of mortgages
foreclosed. Dreams of escape: out of the settled life's
fencerow patrols, into their licensed overthrow:

excess, androgyny, the left wing; anonymity-
celebrity: escape achieved that's no escape,
the waiting misstep, the glassy fjord-leap.

Living anxious. The wind a suicidal howling
in the elevator shaft. The manholes' stinking,
steaming entrails. Dreams, now and again,

lopsided fantasies of going back, weak-kneed,
through the underbrush, and getting even.
One comes to terms, in the long-drawn-out

shadow-war against the old ones: comes
to terms, if one lives long enough, with places
that go strange, that vanish into something else:

is ready to go back, at last, to gravesites, headstones,
the fenced grassland where so many forebears' bones
are boxed and labeled, my grandparents' among them,

my father's and my mother's ashes too. A tranquil
place, unfrightening, now that they rest there:
one comes to terms there, almost, even with dread.

To be landless, half a nomad, nowhere wholly
at home, is to discover, now, an epic theme
in going back. The rootless urge that took

my father's father to Dakota, to California,
impels me there. A settled continent: what
does it mean? I think of nights, half wakeful,

under the roof of their last house, the haven
I knew it as long gone, whoever lives there,
its streetlit solitudes, the clock's tock,

the wooing snuffle of a freight train traveling
along a right of way whose dislodged sleepers now
lie scattered like the bones of mastodons.

I think of Dakota, the wind-raked shelterbelts,
the silos' hived anxiety, the trembling
B-52s. I think of Pasadena: date palms,

hibiscus, pepper trees, the feckless charm
found mainly in the habitat of earthquakes:
half-kempt, aging bungalows gone bridal

under a flowery surfeiting of vines: the desert
fanned, sprinkled, seductive from its bath
of purloined rainbows. North Raymond

not quite a slum; a niggling tenderness
for the outmoded thrives on the scandal
of ways lost, of names gone under. No one

I know or ever heard of lives there now.
On Summit, from some long-obliterated
snapshot, I thought I recognized the house

a great-aunt lived in once: the number
not quite right, the tenant an old
deaf Mexican who did not understand.

from A SILENCE OPENS

(1994)

SYRINX

Like the foghorn that's all lung,
the wind chime that's all percussion,
like the wind itself, that's merely air
in a terrible fret, without so much
as a finger to articulate
what ails it, the aeolian
syrinx, that reed
in the throat of a bird,
when it comes to the shaping of
what we call consonants, is
too imprecise for consensus
about what it even seems to
be saying: is it *o-ka-lee*
or *con-ka-ree*, is it really *jug jug*,
is it *cuckoo* for that matter?—
much less whether a bird's call
means anything in
particular, or at all.

Syntax comes last, there can be
no doubt of it: came last,
can be thought of (is
thought of by some) as a
higher form of expression:
is, in extremity, first to
be jettisoned: as the diva
onstage, all soaring
pectoral breathwork,
takes off, pure vowel
breaking free of the dry,
the merely fricative
husk of the particular, rises
past saying anything, any
more than the wind in

the trees, waves breaking,
or Homer's gibbering
Thespesiae iachē:

those last-chance vestiges
above the threshold, the all-
but dispossessed of breath.

HISPANIOLA

Note how the bear
though armed and dangerous
caring not at all for
dignity, undaintily
snacks on fat white things
paws strawberry meadows
lunges swinging smeared
through blackberry canebrakes
maps a constellated
dream of bee trees
snoring galaxies
the primum mobile
twanging the gulfs
of slumber   beatific
on the tongue
the kiss of honey :
or so we imagine
a hulking innocence
child's-play bedfellow
to the sapient
omnivorous
prehensile
raptor   world-class
bully : the rumor
brought to Alexander
of, in India, a reed
that brought forth honey
sans the help of bees
began it   a topography
of monoculture
blackening the Indus
Tigris-Euphrates
westward-spreading
molasses stain
island plantations
off the coast of
Africa leapfrogging

the Atlantic
Hispaniola
Spanish Mexico
Peru   Paraguay
along the Amazon
the Portuguese
the Dutch   the British
Barbados Antigua Montserrat
Jamaica   huger and huger
deforestations
making way for
raising cane   to be
holed   planted   cut
crushed   boiled
fermented or
reduced to crystalline
appeasement of mammalian
cravings   slave ships
whip-wielding
overseers   world-class
indignity   the bubbling
hellhole of molasses pits
the bear's
(or if not his, whose?)
nightmare

PAUMANOK

The humped, half-subterranean
    potato barns, the tubers
like grown stones, wet meat
    from underground a bused-in,
moved-on proletariat once
    stooped for, where Paumanok's
outwash plain, debris of glaciers,
    frays to a fishtail,

now give place to grapevines,
    their tendency to ramble
and run on, to run to foliage
    curbed, pruned, trained
into another monoculture—row
    after profitable row
on acre after acre, whole landscapes
    strung like a zither

where juniper and honeysuckle,
    bayberry, Virginia creeper,
goldenrod and poison ivy would
    have rioted, the wetlands
glistening at the margin, the reed-
    bed plumes, the groundsel's
tideline windrows a patina of
    perpetual motion

washed by the prevailing airs,
    where driven human
diligence alone could, now or ever,
    undo the uninstructed
thicketing of what keeps happening
    for no human reason,
one comes upon this leeward, mowed
    and tended pocket,

last resting place of slaves, each
grave marked by a boulder
hardly more than a potato's size,
unnamed but as dependents of
Seth Tuthill and his wife Maria,
who chose finally to lie here
with their sometime chattels,
and whose memory too is now
worn down to stone.

MATOAKA

For the tercentenary of the
College of William and Mary

I

Place names, the names of streams—
the Rappahannock, the Roanoke, the Potomac,
and that commemoration of sometime
        majesty, the James,

its tributary the Chickahominy,
the Pamunkey and the Mattaponi, each
what a people called itself once, subsumed in
        a gazetteer, the names

half-overgrown by the long quasi-
anonymity that is history: beyond
the sunken garden, the crape-
        myrtle symmetries,

past the foundation-stone surnames
(Blair, Wythe, Ewell, Brafferton,
Crim Dell), the wooded hillsides,
        in a rippling pause,

the gathered lisp of watersheds,
describe a lake, place-named—
at random, a homage half-absent-
        minded, a penance even?—

Matoaka. A woman's name, though
not the one we know her by,
or imagine we do. To Captain
        John Smith, our own

Odysseus—bright, contentious, crafty,
forever on the move—she'd been
Pocahuntus, well formed but
        wanton, still a child.

Nausicaä, only younger? A king's
daughter as advocate: that was
the story we told once, from which
        we've since recoiled

(we being history) in favor of
the hidden, discreditable motive,
the flagrant fib. Who was she?
        Ask Paul De Man,

for instance. Ask Nietzsche, Freud
or Lévi-Strauss. Ask Parson
Weems, while you're about it.
        Ask any woman

what she thinks, or thought she did.
The stories we tell ourselves keep changing.
Bronze-immobilized, demure in
        deerskin, the heathen

princess turns to bric-a-brac. As
kings' names do. As words—the ritual
twiddle of a once-abrasive contour—
        have also done.

Begin again. Go back to Majesty,
the word personified, a woman:
the dazzlement, the hankering after
        gold, fame, danger,

the smell, the pomandered stink
of it, of her, ruffed, wigged, gemmed,
powdered, breathing, to be adored.
        Back to the courtier

knighted at Greenwich, given leave
to name the shore he claimed, the year
fifteen hundred eighty-four of (mark this)
     our redemption, Vir-

ginia. Such were the forms
and usages, now quaint, of royalty.
Behind them, silences. Silence at
     Roanoke, on the Outer

Banks, what little there ever was
to remember long overgrown: the dunes'
expanse, the largesse of it
     past the unsullied

line of breakers, overrun
with grapevines, sassafras,
the massive green of cedars;
     the white birds, startled,

flying up; an unclad, hospitable
people bringing dressed skins,
the shimmer of a glut of pearls.
     Named Virginia,

a place without detriment or
sleight of language. Households.
Marriages. A girl-child
     named Virginia.

Five years later, footprints.
Ruined walls. A half-carved word.
What happened? By whose fault?
     Silence at Werewo-

comoco, seat of Powhatan,
who—as Captain Smith, his match
in guile, did not forbear to say—
    had his own majesty.

Silence at Henrico, the lands upriver,
and at Varina, where John Rolfe
planted the golden weed that one day
    would amount to money—

Varina, where after many inner
wrestlings, after consultations,
mumblings and catechizings,
    he'd bring his bride,

not as Matoaka or, any longer,
Pocahuntus but, renamed in Christ,
Rebecca. What she called herself
    by then is not recorded.

        2

Christian names, surnames, place names:
Brafferton, called after a manor-
house in Yorkshire, whose rents had been
    bequeathed by Robert Boyle,

a man of learning and great piety,
to bring the infidels of Virginia,
across the water, out of their
    dark and miserable

ignorance to true religion:
Brafferton, a monument
to words we, or some of us,
    once listened to

in fear and trembling: divinity,
hell fire, the Fiend, Redemption,
Eternal Judgment: Brafferton,
        monument at last to

policy, tergiversation and
neglect. What happened? Whose
fault was it few gave credence to
        the awesome news

of Love personified, Who, having
undergone the worst, might still
prove to outlast undoing? Awe,
        in all the stories

we tell ourselves, is finally
what's durable, no matter how
we mollify it, no matter how our
        pieties keep changing.

What happened in the mind of John
Smith's nonpareil, a pagan
without a peer, grown nubile,
        then the shining

jewel of imperial endeavor,
now the mere sullied pawn
of statecraft and testosterone,
        who dares imagine?

After what dazzlements, what
threats, what stirred, fearful
increment of passion, as Mistress
        Rolfe, she crossed

that threshold, who can guess?
Concerning what she thought, miasmas,
quagmires, white birds flying up,
    the Holy Ghost,

deter us. Who's the more lost?
She had, at any rate, her uses.
Newly installed as convert, nursing
    mother and great lady

up the river named for his
increasingly unseemly majesty,
see her embark, chief showpiece
    of colonial bravado.

Now records of a sort begin:
of presentations, masques, levees,
of portrait sittings, wearing
    wig, ruff, mantle

of brocaded velvet; no less,
for a season, than the rage
of foul, fashionable London
    with its spiteful

stares and whispers, its catarrhs,
its bruited rifts and ruinings,
the whole interminable,
    fatiguing catalog

of latest things, the gartered
glitterings, the breathing
propinquity of faces: through
    a pomandered fog

of rooms and posturings arises,
stunningly vivid still yet
dim with distance, a figure
    long gone from Jamestown,

an ocean's retching, heaving
vertigo removed, and more: from
girlhood's remembered grapevines,
    strawberries, sun-

warm mulberries, leapfrog,
cartwheels, the sound of streams,
of names, of languages: Pamunkey,
    Chickahominy . . .

She'd thought him dead. She'd never
been so tired. There in London
a silence opens: Captain Smith,
    repenting to have writ she

could speak English, is witness
of how she turned away—she who,
out of a distance grown by now
    intolerable, had seen

the world, so called: brought face
to face with majesty, with empire, by
. that silence she took their measure.
    Amicably, then,

she acknowledged him, and Jamestown;
as for his countrymen (in what tone
and with what gesture?), they were a people
    that often lied.

Details are few. At Gravesend, readying
for the crossing, aged twenty-one,
she seemingly abruptly
        sickened and died.

3

The chancel of St. George's, Gravesend,
gave her Christian burial. That she
would have chosen this we are less certain,
        given our own

tergiversations, the worn-down
pieties we stumble over,
that trip us up—gnarled rootstocks
        of the once counted on,

knobbed, knotted stubs, newer-
than-kudzu cure-alls, defunct
cultures—silk and indigo,
        the golden weed

King James once railed against
(correctly, it latterly appears)
as noxious, till persuaded there was
        money to be made:

tobacco money, sometime mainstay
of a college given royal grant
and charter to propagate a faith
        the courtier Raleigh,

having staked a last flirtatious
toss, and lost it, in
the shadowy predatory tentshow
        we know as history,

declared for: from beyond this earth,
this grave, this dust (he wrote)
the Lord would raise him up. Such was
      his trust. Less certain,

ourselves, of anything except
the omniprevalence of error,
here on the claimed soil of (in
      the words of Drayton,

who never saw it) earth's
only paradise, to stroll
beyond the commemorated
      names of Brafferton,

Blair, Wythe, Ewell, past
Crim Dell, down to where
mere water, rippling, preserves
      the name of one—

her true, her secret name perhaps,
but that's surmise—the world has heard of,
of whom we know so little: to stroll thus
      is to move nearer,

in imagination, to the nub,
the pulse, the ember of what she was—
no stranger, finally, to the mystery
      of what we are.

SHOREBIRD-WATCHING

To more than give names
to these random arrivals—
teeterings and dawdlings
of dunlin and turnstone,
black-bellied or golden
plover, all bound for

what may be construed as
a kind of avian Althing
out on the Thingstead,
the unroofed synagogue
of the tundra—is already
to have begun to go wrong.

What calculus, what
tuning, what unparsed
telemetry within the
retina, what overdrive
of hunger for the nightlong
daylight of the arctic,

are we voyeurs of? Our
bearings gone, we fumble
a welter of appearance,
of seasonal plumages
that go dim in winter:
these bright backs'

tweeded saffron, dark
underparts the relic
of what sibylline
descents, what harrowings?
Idiot savants, we've
brought into focus

such constellations,
such gamuts of
errantry, the very
terms we're condemned
to try to think in
turn into a trespass.

But Adam, drawn toward
that dark underside,
its mesmerizing
circumstantial thumbprint,
would already have
been aware of this.

GREEN

These coastal bogs, before they settle
    down to the annual
business of being green, show an
    ambivalence, an overtone

halfway autumnal, half membranous
    sheen of birth: what is
that cresset shivering all by itself
    above the moss, the fallen duff—

a rowan? What is that gathering blush
    of russet the underbrush
admits to—shadblow, its foliage
    come of ungreen age?

The woods are full of this, the red
    of an anticipated
afterglow that's (as it were) begun
    in gore, green that no more than

briefly intervenes. More brief
    still is the whiff,
the rime, the dulcet powdering, just now,
    of bloom that for a week or two

will turn the sullen boglands airy—
    a look illusory
of orchards, but a reminder also
    and no less of falling snow.

Petals fall, leaves hang on all
    summer; chlorophyll,
growth, industry, are what they hang
    on for. The relinquishing

of doing things, of being occupied
    at all, comes hard:
the drifting, then the lying still.

THE HORNED RAMPION

Daily, out of that unfamiliar,
entrancingly perpendicular
terrain, some new
and, on minute
inspection, marvelous
thing would be opening—

yet another savory-
flowery permutation
of selene or salvia,
of scabious, of rockrose,
of evening primrose, of
bellflower such as the one

I'd never before laid eyes
on the like of: spurred,
spirily airy, a sort of
stemborne baldachin,
a lone, poised,
hovering rarity, hued

midway between the clear
azure of the rosemary
and the aquilegia's
somberer purple,
that turned out to be
named the horned rampion.

Next day it was no longer
singular but several;
the day after, many.
Within a week it was
everywhere, had become
the mere horned rampion,

had grown so familiar
I forgot it, had not
thought of it since,
it seems, until the moment
a volume of the Encyclopedia
Britannica, pulled down

for some purpose, fell open
at random, and there was
the horned rampion, named
and depicted, astonishing
in memory as old love
reopened, still quivering.

IN UMBRIA: A SNAPSHOT

The coldest, wettest spring within living memory
is the way they describe it. At Assisi
there have been six straight weeks of rain.
They blame it on the Gulf War, of which Melina
happily, for the time being, knows nothing.
A vehement "*Good*ness!" is her fiercest expletive.

Little runaway, forget-me-not-eyed, ringlet-
aureoled refugee from a fresco by Lorenzetti—
all those gold-leaf rigors, the theological
murk underneath—whom nobody can begin to
keep up with, or anyhow nobody human. *Her*
peers are the brown-faced saint's familiars:

he of the caninely grinning lope, they of
the barnyard strut and chuckle, the noon-hour
flurry, by the recycled temple of Minerva, of
brakings and hoverings, structure and function
of wingbeats she'd been gleefully part of
minutes before going romping off into a dark

she knows nothing about—or is one, at a year
and eight months, already prey to nightmares?—
that goes back to before the Gulf War. *"La bimba!"*—
the reverberation accused us along the catacomb
she stood crying in, consoled by who knows, by now,
how many strangers: Kodachromed all over Umbria

beaming, the crowd scene in the café or the square
perceived as benediction, one unendingly
extended family: or come to a halt, as now,
halfway up an impossible hill, aware of being
small and alone: incipience a spinning globe
(look! the sun's out), all its great spaces opening.

BIRDHAM

Hemmed by loud seas,
by fractured granite, by island
treescapes each spined like a hedgehog,
as well as wild roses' formidable
coppices, on beholding
an up-late-in-daylight
porcupine, its thicketed
shambling perpendicular a stupor
of armament, I thought

of Birdham, all meek horizontals,
blurred margins, sea meeting land
among lanes and hedgerows:
of mild, tall, approachable
roses and delphiniums, a robin
scavenging the tablecloth at
teatime: of exclaiming, one evening,
"Barbara, there's a hedgehog
out in the garden!"

"Oh," my friend complacently
said then, "that's Henry."
Far-off, long-settled
Birdham is like that.

MANHATTAN

For Phoebe Hoss

GRACE CHURCH

A day of gusts and puddles, the vivid
litter of a season no better ordered
than the debris we carry with us, each,

of hurt and counter-hurt, attachments
wrenched from or slowly shed, engulfs
the maudlin fretwork, the pieced glass.

Like kids, unwilling, sent back to school,
we learn how our own history has its exits
and its entrances, its waning phase.

Once, even the wry sendoff to Reno
seemed expansive; the mists and gustings
of champagne, the shipboard trysts,

slip now into the backward and abysm
with the mortgage burnings, tinkling
martini pitchers on the beach at Gilgo;

Southold with its steamer clams, beer
and garrulity; the boozeless week at
Flynn's—Fire Island beach fires,

sunsets on Great South Bay; birthday
bashes, welcomes home, milestone
observances assembling yet again

the loose, patched, decades-frayed,
half-accidental, half-willed Old Crowd.
Habitual molecules have their gatherings

and dispersals: we learn how our,
how every history comes down to
this, the encounter with the starved

handclasp from the wheelchair: to share
the bed of this, seeing it distend,
begin to ooze like an edema: death,

that blear-eyed, feathery noise. He'd
kept a careful regimen—no alcohol,
a daily six-mile run—had coaxed

a rooftop lotus into bloom, thrown
memorable parties. An *Augenblick*
through tokay lampshade-glades,

trompe-l'oeil and calfskin: fey connoisseur
of the unlooked-for (the diagnosis:
cancer of the liver) sharing tête-à-tête

a glimpse he'd noted as he ran: in
Central Park, through early-morning
mist, a surreptitious crew of women,

unmistakably Chinese, with raised
poles harvesting the dun produce
of a stand of ginkgo trees. An

eyeblink of the hand-to-hand, the
elfin bubble of the incorporeal
settles, shivering, as the mind is stilled.

CHARLES STREET

Transplanted from the Carolinas, from
Pittsfield and Sewickley, the raw demes
of Appalachia and Iowa, from the arterio-

sclerotic clot across the Hudson, among
the walkups, the ginkgo-shaded side streets
of Greenwich Village, to claim the privilege

of ignoring one's next-door neighbors, of
getting drunk in bars, of being sick in
hallways, of fornications in strange beds,

solipsist terrors of the mad, the marginal,
the merely totally confused—we'd come
to listen for the West Side Highway's

nightlong silken seethe, for foghorns
mourning the tenor of the day before it
opened, for subliminal harmonic tremors

as the old *Queen Mary* cleared her larynx;
to spy out trivial marvels in mundane
bazaars: I think of the Fourteenth Street

refreshment stand whose reamers gushed,
one balefully faceless fall, with juices
not of crushed citrus or papaya, but

of crammed red-parchment pomegranates'
casefuls of rubies, each with its nucleus
of possibility encysted at the center,

translucent hemoglobin of exotic groves
adrift among dead-end chicaneries, bins
of cut-rate merchandise, all-weather

scavengers of trashcans, the misfit
solitaries, dislocated extended families
from Puerto Rico, the dwindling remnant

of the native Irish. From symbiotic
venoms of achieve or be undone, the candor
of whatever community distilled its own

scarce nostrum finds a remembered center
in gatherings, the back garden lantern-
strung, on Charles Street, where from

occasion to occasion a mazy entity affirmed
itself in loose sendoff talk of ashrams,
of reunions so exotic, the sheer prospect

so like a gem I'd wear it home
and watch it turn into the dawn, an opal's
packed circumference: nowhere to stash it

but in the scuffed insomniac luggage
of a future lately overpast. The scions
of a new uprooting gather now, or wake alone

and scared, on Charles Street; the ginkgos'
bare, bud-nubbed brooms purvey the wizened
gemstones of a dun, unasked-for fruit.

THE STATEN ISLAND FERRY

December, and again an exit, the slow
aftershock of months-old news (inoperable
cancer of the pancreas). At Grace Church

the day after the equinox, we'd seen him
wheeled in starving, the awful door
blown to. Today, a half-involuntary

particle in the shifting habitual
concourse that floods the gangway
as the slung barrier recedes, to board

the shunted, hooting, double-snub-
nosed tub he was as much at home in as
an owned house (he'd been a seaman,

had the lover of precision's ear
for discord; for him, unjaded by
familiarity, it was as though the harbor

could do no wrong), is to feel the stale
hour lose its nerve, grow listless, slip,
marked only, if at all, by some braced

gull's half-obliterated outcry, toward
the solstice: toward the annual foreboding of
a swerve, this year, through outer cold

no longer to be bridged. Hart Crane's
great cabled lyre corrodes: a frayed
strand one day broke, dangled, struck

and killed between the boroughs' apoplectic
upthrust and wrecking claw, the stunned
queue, the gusted, elbowing guffaws,

True Believers in the sanctity of Wear
and Tear, the quaint ordeal of Trickle-Down,
a continent, a people, a consensus unmoored

from any history at all—the whole mythic
mishegass that used him up. Asked why
he shrugged—he shrugged a lot, drank

still more, grew more and more low-
key—he would have murmured, "Is there
a better system, then?" The fossil carbon

of whatever outrage still smoldered in the
wreckage, that fall day, we turned away from.
Beside the stripped carapace of Ellis Island,

gowned Liberty in effigy lofts her
Promethean fable on the decades-sodden
pilings, bile and verdigris—crass icon

of the possible, the yet-, the never-to-be-
ventured-on. From the railing he'd drink in
this daily brew of hubris and sea air

as from a stein. The random particles
disbanding, the estuarial currents merge:
the mind gropes toward its own recessional.

'EIGHTY-NINE

In memory of Andrew Myers

Season of contaminated mists,
    of premises abandoned, the heartland
curdling in a spate of messages—
    the sequined smirk, the flicker
of apocalypse only the young, whose
    prospects who cares to imagine,
        can stand to dance to:
    season of scavengers: how is it,
in the evening light above the landfill
the gulls, massed, hovering, diaphanous,
    take on the look of angels?

John Keats at Winchester, fair-weather
    scavenger of what pleases the eye,
was for the nonce persuaded by just
    such appearances: the stubblefields
suffused, the season's lineaments
    discerned as halfway human. Time
        equivocates: though no epiphany
    outstays the wholly dividual rupture,
above the water meadows' jewelweed and
fennel the midge-swarm hangs, its scrim
    untorn, as without interruption.

Continuity of the winged, the windborne,
    the rooted: reassurance of the made,
the handed down, the durable: glyph
    and vesper bell, trodden cloister and
walled playing field: it was as though,
    that evening, the young athletes
        in their perfect whites, the bat's
    pock, the patter of applause—as though
pure sport had turned the key against
fever and shivering, nausea, hemorrhage,
    the entire obscenity of dying young.

O, or of dying at any age, by degrees
    or by accident: to be alive at all
is no more than an ambuscade, eluding
    the presence of angels, since it is
in the nature of angels to be terrible:
    thralled to the heavings of a visceral
        mass peepholed with ganglia,
    while somewhere in there the big-eyed rabbit
of delirium, cowering, scared witless, waits:
O dense as spiders' spinning trajectories
    at summer's end are these inklings

of undoing; or as the seasonal downpour
    distends to a cording of thongs and sinews,
a knout of wet one gives oneself up to,
    soaked through, having made one's peace with
whatever the elements can do. Or almost.
    For beyond that peace is the shape of
        calamity nobody is ever
    ready for: on a day at the end of summer,
a car going off the road, a mangling
incendiary gasp, and for four young athletes,
    without harbinger all is over.

He was twenty, the one I knew: T-shirted,
    dripping from the shower is the way
I remember him, just passing through. Such
    images console somehow. When the note came,
with the clipping, I saw the capacity for grief
    sit there, in the face of such cautery, inert
        with refusal. But the mother
    had already entered (as she'd later put it)
a place where the things people do for one
have no names: such an inrush, she lived floating
    in a deep lake of it, of that charity.

Mourning her own unborn, uncosseted
    grandchildren, she'd have gone over and over
the lack of evidence of design in the event,
    having met with the messengers, having
found them (and even the archangels are,
    after all, only messengers) inscrutable.
        O how intricate a patterning
    in the bracken's yellowing diminishment,
the hornet's fallen factories; in the squirrel's
uncalculated leap a smoke-ring wavelength's
    theorem still fluttering.

What, then, notwithstanding the evidence
    of dance at the heart of the matter,
whatever matter may be, of all the arson
    and concussion, of that blister they call
the Sea of Tranquillity? What of the atom,
    its core no dance hall but a regardless
        demos, disaster's hotbed?
    For all our jargon of knowing and managing,
for all our summoning of the forces of order,
in a season of sour rain, how happily
    we looked at anarchy in bloom.

Strange, what a year it was altogether
    for anniversaries—all the might-have-
beens of human nature seemingly reborn;
    of, even, that November weekend—
the all-night bus ride, the carried candles,
    an exuberance of rage over being lied to,
        and the out-of-season rose
    that turned into an epiphany: in
that uprush of forces, of faces, the anarchic
sweetness of it (it was twenty years
    ago) I had my youth again.

Youth, in Tiananmen Square, arriving just
    ahead of the great anniversary: was it
evidence of design in the weft of things,
    that legion of messengers, headband-
wearers at once lighthearted and terrible,
        as all angels are? O insomniac
            loveliness of arrival, of
        exposure to the downpours of summer,
to the far, forgetful stars, those envoys
of long-undergone concussions, O insouciance
    in the face of the forces of order.

Candlelight on the cobblestones of Leipzig;
    in Prague a complicit candor, as night
after night we were drawn to the tube
    (O brute honey, there in the dark,
though the smirk of mendacity contain it)
    by the flowering, out in the snow, of so
        many faces: now that season's over.
    But that freshet of anarchy,
while it lasted, halfway persuaded us
the archangels, whoever they are,
    at moments are also human.

AT MUKER, UPPER SWALEDALE

To be wet was to be captive, idle and poor. To be dry was to be free, industrious and comfortable. This was the lesson of the drowning cell.

SIMON SCHAMA, *The Embarrassment of Riches*

The farmer with his milk pail
pausing, a fine rain falling,
burnishing with wet the wind-
nipped roof slates, fingering
the chimney-clumps of dwellings

following no plan or pattern
but that of having sat down,
one by one, as sheep would,
in the moor's high, wall-
ribbed, uncomfortable lee:

so it appears to one come as,
though country bred, a stranger,
to trudge the solitude of footpaths,
then early bed and, out of rural
sleep, dreams that are frantic

as Muker Beck aswirl, hurtling
to enter the River Swale: peat-
dark in spate, hour by hour
engorged with braidings, with
sheeted seethings of rainfall

fallen yet again: the trickle
of the damp's wrung increment
down limestone's fluted hollows
(buttertubs is what the locals
call them) that pock the pass

along the road to Askrigg—
slow, muted, single droplets
like bird notes after dark,
filterings ringleted with
brunet-stemmed spleenwort,

ageless as the lamb's cry,
the bees' noise, the lisp
of aeons. Strange, the lone
lapwing, the streamside fox-
glove, the harebell by the

roadside, the pale-eyed piebald
Swaledale breed, met up with
in one knockdown gathering,
the herdsman's yell (*Git in,
git in, git in, ye buggers*),

the neat small sheepdog doing
what it's bred for, all strange—
even the farmer's quasi-gentlemanly
tweed and Wellingtons: it's only
the milk pail takes me back to

the matriarchal smell of it,
warm from the udder; to manure-
pile, barnyard and stanchion,
green reek of silage, green
scum on the horse-trough,

year-round wall-sweat of old
farmhouses; to pump, sink,
cistern, slop pail for pigs,
the human slop jar, the gray
interminable hank of mildew.

Well, that's changing. Indoor
shivers give way (even here,
now that the heating's central)
to plush, florid wall-to-wall,
rippling fake fire, the daylong

warbling of the telly; to a
comfort wishfully aspired
toward, become no more than
the way we all—or if not all,
then most, or if not most,

the icons of our surrogate
existence—live now. Think,
though, of that roamer in the
rainy deserts of this shire,
the never-to-be-comfortable

George Fox, sworn enemy of
easy livings, of the steeple-
house's dry doldrums—who,
acquainted with the stink of
anybody in a state of nature,

a prisoner wading ankle-deep
in excrement, envisioning
beyond these elements a
heavenly rain descending,
aspired toward pure fire.

SED DE CORRER

Caught on the move—no knowing what year it was—
through the leaves of the ash tree outside the schoolroom,
the stumbling drone, the ineradicable blush, the botch
of being young: O how can I breathe, the eyes
are all mouths, they are drinking me—that glimpse:
a small bird, some part of it, among streakings
and shadings, the fluttering fan of it, afire
(a Blackburnian warbler? I ask myself now:
a redstart?) uncaught by the impeding
rigors of the vascular, the cambium's moist secrets
locked between xylem and phloem, the great, growing
trunk of it hardening, the mass, the circumference,
the unhurried, implacably already
there, that's to be escaped from:

escape, the urge to disjoin, the hunger
to have gone, to be going: *sed de correr:*
Vallejo in Paris writing (*me alejo todo*)
of fleeing, of running away from what made one,
from everything: Lorca, a stranger to
Morningside Heights, looking out from
that ridge above Harlem: the mire and fireflies,
the lit grid's apertures past counting,
the bleared eyeholes of jails: the tiered rictus
at Creedmore and Brentwood, where the mad
are warehoused, who do not look out of,
who burrow, denying the need for,
the nature and function, the very existence
of windows: holed up torpid, hibernal,
one day possibly (or possibly never),
fluttering, desiccated, frail,
to emerge from that hebetude:

the runaway halt, no opening other than
the starry apertures of paperwhite narcissus
forced in a bowl, cool, onion-rooted,
a sweetness I drank at as though entity

might depend from it: exploring
chlorinated caves of sensation (wet hair,
wool-steam, the pipes knocking), away from
the blare, out there, of certitude,
the glare of injunction: meaning
dwindling to a risen chain of bubbles
in the saucepan on the hotplate: the hurrying
fin far out, the lighthouse,
its pulsing aperture engulfed,
the waves breaking.

Virginia Woolf, having written her note of farewell,
going down to the river, the largest stone
she could manage shoved into her pocket: the body
of Lorca crumpling, shot down at the edge of
a pit on the outskirts of Granada: Vallejo
in Paris, in extremis, crying out on Good Friday
A.D. 1938, "I'm going to Spain!"—pulled up,
cut off from his own roots' torment,
the certitudes, the incursions, the plunder:
having written of the condition of cities,
of being alone among people: the windows looked out of,
the mute telephone, the dementia: Kafka
devising a passage up through the windowless
warren of calculation, contingency, foresight
there's no way out of, metamorphosing
escape in the form—O no, not of a bird,
not he who so fled the open, but of an insect
gravitating unerringly toward the dark:
those feelers, that lustrous, chitinous
lodging among interstices, among systems
we've lost track of the workings of,
and to whose advantage, outwitting
the gathering impasse of language, the screech
of its decibels, the mumble of its circumlocutions,
the mutter, all over Europe, of what sooner and sooner
was bound, was about to happen.

Refugees were arriving. Cut off, adrift, at large
in the fathomless afternoon of arrival,
alone—suppose that to be seen by no one
would be in fact to vanish?—I looked out from
a window ledge on Morningside Heights,
that ridge overlooking the eyesore
of real estate that is Harlem, too scared
to begin to grapple with, to think in
the inexorable terms of, the leverages
of excuse that maintained it: impervious
to the ideologue's whereases and necessarilys,
the thunderous because, the sad, lingering
cadenza of notwithstanding, I was not deaf to
the screech of what had somehow knowably—
how?—been closing in, closing down
ever since I'd begun to remember. Refugees:
it was with a refugee I'd venture,
just once, into Harlem: Jan Muller, who'd later,
vividly, paint his way through an insomniac
excess while he died of it, like Kafka. Refugees:
from the songless amputated tree
Lorca wrote of: leaves fallen, adrift,
the great trunk lost sight of, the stasis
of such scattering, such dispersals.

Adrift among hallways, stairwells, airshafts,
the asphalt of rooftops, among old-law walkups,
the rusting entablatures, fire escapes'
catfoot walkways, upended avenues of thievery,
of escape that is no escape: trailing the shuddering
jointed lurch alongside the platform, elevated
or submerged, the serial unseeing faces
within, the windows traveling, a delirium of them,
of arrivals, escapes that are no escape: cheap
plane tickets from Puerto Rico—to what? Rooftop
rainwater weeping in, the aerials, the hutches
put up by breeders of pigeons: the wild rock dove's
cosmopolitan offspring, their homing swerve

more nearly adapted than these refugees
from the canefields' corridored, murderous green,
caught up in the wingborne roar, the breaking
wave of displacement—so many injunctions
in need of translation—translated here, to
the crass miracle of whatever it is that put up
the South Bronx, street number after street number,
the mailbox pried open, recipient unknown,
moved on, shot down—and has made of it
this byword, this burnt-out, roofless, windowless
testimonial to systems gone rotten.
This arson.

There is much too much to be done: so Vallejo,
a wistful sometime disciple of Lenin,
declared: but who heard him? Not I,
shades drawn against being seen, against systems,
from bohemia's sempiternal cocoon, the hallways
smelling of cat piss and mildew. Who will hear?
Rilke wondered, imagining the rush from out there,
the vast presences, harsh with transcendence,
whose nature it is to ignore one. Not those great wings.
I was too much afraid. By a window
onto an airshaft one night I stood awed
at the sight of two men making love. I'd not
known how it was done. Through thin walls,
year after year, I could not stop up my ears to
the spats, the crudities, the climaxes
faked or unfaked, to (once) the squalled outcry
while others came to the rescue. What
my ears awaited, out past the suicidal refuge
of a fire escape on West Twelfth Street,
was the all-but-inaudible, the lisped *tsip,*
in a back-garden catalpa, the fluttering fan
of a warbler on the move: spring or fall,
that glimpsed inkling of things
beyond systems, windborne, oblivious.

Sed de correr: above Tijuana, where the language,
its streams and islets, begins to change color,
the moiling crawl along the freeway—
la cucaracha, the refuge of Gregor Samsa
writ large, written everywhere—a teenage
entrepreneur selling roses, bull's-blood-
red velvet of a piece with all the matador
kitsch across the border, threading the labyrinth
of the need to flee, to be at once on the go
and in hiding, that's what we've become.
The moving vehicle. The estrangement.
On West Twelfth Street, the tree is dying:
the rough, green-napped, huge heart shapes,
the cigar shapes, the striations at the throat
of the ruffled corolla, year by year, are
expiring by inches. The axe is laid
at the root of the ash tree. The leaves of dispersal,
the runaway pages, surround us. Who
will hear? Who will gather
them in? Who will read them?

MATRIX
(Villa Serbelloni, Lake Como)
For Karen Chase

Perched for the nonce among such verticals,
such strata (And did the Principessa
have any friends down there?—O no,

she was *nobilità*), where history
is one long redoubt, where underlings
daily feed into the mangle, fold

on fold, the vellum-and-magnolia-petal
linens we sleep between—our dreams
burrow toward bedrock, down to the matrix,

as though the flinging open of so many
windows, such excess of light and air,
of attitude, the ease of bearing

up from the crypt, encysted, lapidary,
such indignities—the plucked eyeball
of Saint Lucy, Saint Roch's leprous thigh,

Sebastian, his lovely nakedness a grove,
a garden of undoing; the gouging
and the piercing, the vials held

by winged minions frantic lest a drop,
a berry from the tree of earthly horror
go unaccounted for; the ooze of blood,

O hideous, O precious—could not
but be requited by some warden of
the long-repressed, exhuming this

wrapped corpse: holy and dreadful,
the undisposed-of body of the mother.
Whose? The nightmare is not being sure.

Down by the lake we note, strolling a dense
memorial clutter, the dead baby, starkly
photographed; wreathed and embedded,

la moglie in mourning overhung
by the carved smirk of an upstart
lord and master; faceless in their nook

outside the walls, the name and birthplace
of the Englishman who drowned, whose fate
now furnishes the stony living-room

we who still live inhabit: outcrop and under-
croft, retaining wall where lizards hide,
the red valerian hangs, and busy daisies

here called *margherite* burgeon in
a sun the cool spleenwort shrinks from;
precipice in whose still deeper shade

the violets of spring live on, as though
they'd undermine the summer; stone,
nurturer of Europe, the bereaved

exile's lost mother—otherwise
why this going back, these hankerings
after a relinquished privilege,

why her indentured hold on what we are
or could have been, why this unearned
nostalgia for the culture of the vine,

the pruning of the olive? Observing
how a laborer with a scythe, his
immemorial bending curve repeated

all afternoon, turned what had been a meadow
stippled first with buttercups, then the
beginning red of poppies, into a hayfield,

I thought (don't laugh) of Virgil
brooding on unrest in the metropolis,
knowing the countryside to be no idyl—

one's neighbors sly and fickle, played on
by superstitious rant. Some things
hardly change. There came an evening

toward the end of May, the cherries
reddening on the slope, when a small
procession, mainly of women, moved

up through the hayfield to a chapel
built in honor of My, Our, Their
Lady of the Montserrato, as every year

it had for, in this instance, precisely
the last four hundred. Some of us
came down (ah, feudal perquisites)

from dinner to look on. The Lady,
it appears, was Spanish to begin with,
named for a place denoting merely

a serrated peak. And so, above
her altar the Holy Child is shown
with, in his little hand, a little saw.

What *is* all this? Vigil candles
were fluttering; rosary-fingerers,
swaying as they sang, were singing

over and over, "Ave Maria, Madre di
Dio, tu sei la madre della Chiesa"—and
if, swaying with them, the pagan thrill

I felt had in it something wistful,
the thing I hankered after was no
rite but a foundation, the bedrock

that survives, the banded strata,
hurled reliquary of the drowned,
remnant of uncountable transformings:

precipice, gray limestone I've looked up
into the face of until the looking up
amounted to an attitude of worship:

stone that rings underfoot, whose surfaces
grow populous within doors as a tuned
instrument, eloquent of what lived once,

is now the stuff of cliffs, of crypts,
of hideaways. This morning, following
a track down to the lake, I came upon

a hollow in the cliff wall where,
drip-eroded, rosary-hung, dead flowers
littering the cave floor, there she was:

prayed to and put upon, another idol
of the universal mother. What *is*
all this? The infant in us still

won't let her go—lugubrious poppet,
nurturer, devourer: down below,
well-being's amniotic nightmare

still rocking to its own small music,
cradling the precipice—the clear,
uneasy, treacherous green water.

A SILENCE

past parentage or gender
beyond sung vocables
the slipped-between
the so infinitesimal
fault line
a limitless
interiority

beyond the woven
unicorn   the maiden
(man-carved   worm-eaten)
God at her hip
incipient
the untransfigured
cottontail
bluebell and primrose
growing wild   a strawberry
chagrin   night terrors
past the earthlit
unearthly masquerade

(we shall be changed)

a silence opens

§

the larval feeder
naked   hairy   ravenous
inventing from within
itself its own
raw stuffs'
hooked silk-hung
relinquishment

behind the mask
the milkfat   shivering
sinew   isinglass
uncrumpling   transient
greed to reinvest

§

names have been
given   (revelation
kif   nirvana
syncope)   for
whatever gift
unasked
gives birth to

torrents
fixities
reincarnations of
the angels
Joseph Smith
enduring
martyrdom

a cavernous
compunction driving
founder-charlatans
who saw in it
the infinite
love of God
and had
(George Fox
was one)
great openings

UNCOLLECTED POEMS

Excerpts from THE SUN ON THE STONE

"The Sun on the Stone" is an unpublished poem begun after Amy Clampitt experienced a religious insight during a visit to The Cloisters in New York City in 1956. The revelation, and the composition of the poem by a writer who thought of herself as a novelist, is described in a long letter to a brother, Philip Clampitt, dated March 17, 1956. Reproduced in *Love, Amy: The Selected Letters of Amy Clampitt* (edited by Willard Spiegelman, 2005), that account can be seen as the most important surviving letter of Clampitt's life. There she isolates her witnessing of sunlight on stone as her moment of Christian conversion, and confides simultaneously her confidence that she belongs in the roll call of English literature. Yet not long after showing this poem, or a draft of it, to a friend who did not receive it well, Clampitt apparently stopped writing poetry for years.

In this poem, she salutes as if they were saints many writers important to her: Henry Adams, John Keats, William Wordsworth, Gerard Manley Hopkins, Oswald Spengler, D. H. Lawrence, Henry James, Virginia Woolf, Katherine Mansfield, Marcel Proust, and Sophocles. She alludes to both Milton and Dante. T. S. Eliot is not mentioned, but his poems are clearly an important influence on the poem's more modern moments.

"The Sun on the Stone" is an everything-but-the-kitchen-sink of a poem, and much of it is apprentice work written with a stiff high-mindedness. Knowledge is good, fear is to be avoided ("Seek not henceforth to shun / knowing . . ."). The passages below offer some beautifully turned lines, however, and they reveal some key themes not only in this poem but also in the poetic career that would follow many years later.

Interestingly, a poem with a similar title, "The Sun Underfoot Among the Sundews," would be her first work published in *The New Yorker.* That whimsical poem of 1978 considers a "First Cause," "that backhand, round- / about refusal to assume responsibility / known as Natural Selection." "The Sun on the Stone" also introduces the myth of Medusa—the Gorgon who turned men to stone—that would be central to Clampitt's third book, *Archaic Figure,* three decades hence.

The poem is eighteen typed pages long, and divided into seven titled sections Clampitt did not number: (1) Prologue: Outside Limbo; (2) The Garden of the Unicorn; (3) The Gardens of Purgatory; (4) The Invocation; (5) The Recessional; (6) The Descent and the Return to the Unreal; and (7) The Mysteries of Incandescence.

Reproduced here are parts of sections 1, 3, 5, and 7.

THE SUN ON THE STONE

Ma qui la morta poesì resurga,
o sante Muse, poi che vostro sono
PURGATORIO, I, 7–8

I. PROLOGUE: OUTSIDE LIMBO

Drowned in the disembodiment of light
The river rumbles unbelievable
Below a parapet of broom and heather;
Impending shadows bruise the Palisades
While strollers, undone by neither
The unfound nor the irretrievable,
Despite the unseasonable weather
(For in the shade
Of rock and rhododendron the quaint shock
Of snow yet quivers,
And unremarked
The icy thaw-drip tinkles, darkening the stonecrop ledges)
Are undone, are dismayed,
Strolling above the swollen, the incomprehensible river,
Only by the moist, bland, barely conceivable,
Anonymous, discommoding light—
Light that penetrates the will and thaws the edges
Of the separate self, that to know itself requires the accommodation of the dark.

[. . .]

Pseudo St. Denis, bearing his severed head
And weary of a climb he never made
Except to please the gullible, prefers to leave us moderately aghast
Rather than speak mysteries that may not be transplanted.

For see, in the false cloistered turf the crocuses
Have fallen on their faces,
The anemones are forced, the squills are stunted,
The gardener is all too fallible; growth is affronted
By millionaires' and curators' careful trespasses
And niggling violence upon the past.
The pseudo-Grail has yielded its precarious, lambent tarnish
To the scrubbings of Hollywood and the furious
Varnishing roar of the color presses:
We are left not even curious.

Why on earth did we come?
Now that the reliquaries are shorn
Of their bones, now that the wooden
Worm-eaten bishops fail to be mysterious
And the maiden
With God at her hip is dumb,
Now that God, finally worn
Out by repeated dyings and resurrections, has retired
(Could He, scared, only have hidden?),
Or absconded, or resolved into atoms of air,
Have we come here
Merely to stroke a tame dragon, gape at a gilded Spanish angel, or admire
A sky from the workshop of Rogier van der Weyden?

For whatever ultimate purpose we were born
It can hardly have been to look at a tapestry unicorn.

3. THE GARDENS OF PURGATORY

[. . .]

The sun moves down the stone; upon the molten river
Light clangs as from a forge;
Gulls dip quicksilver; before the winnowing thunder,
The soundless scourge,
On river and roadway the merely mechanical mumbles, rasps, and goes under.

Light shall purge
All being: light is the final judge.
Emerging faith

The rain of truth
Shall scald like wrath
At the day of revelation.

Surprised in their preoccupation
By dazzlement, the pair on the ramparts shiver
Whether at the beginning of the final conflagration
They do not know: but for the moment they have lost each other; they cannot see; while
   below them the traffic whirrs
With a whisper of chaff; and behind them the bridge's stretched spans quiver
Like a fall of gossamers.

    5. THE RECESSIONAL

[...]

Pillared Sophocles,
Across the frozen
Portal of whose lunar pity the actuality
Of our exhumed, unshriven terror
Stalked: who showed an antique horror turned to stone,
Before his time, a suffering serenity

[...]

    7. THE MYSTERIES OF INCANDESCENCE

[...]

Fear of encountering reflection
In the multitudinous, mirroring solitudes of drawing-room propriety
Is the ice
In the arteries
Of every congealed convention.

Every crime and vice
Every petrifying turpitude
Sprang from the head,
The Medusa stare
Of fear.

[...]

THE EQUINOCTIAL DISTURBANCES

the gusts and gutterings
will have given way
to hovering particles of the
great blank   the colorless
all-color

looked out upon   the snowlit
iron memorials
enclose a rumor of
already undergone
rehearsals

the putting off
of ordinary deprivations
to be enrobed   as for
a festival   in
the same dazzle

as (O splendor of re-
appearances) the streamside
bloodroot   the whitening
cherry trees along
the park drive

cheekily eloquent
even the livid
roadside comedian   flicks
its chevrons' white
the wingpatch

a mime of those
prodigious beckonings
one somehow (how?)
might rise to the
occasion of

Pain Management arrives
dressed all in green
a rosebud in (can morphine
have invented this?)
its buttonhole

Oncology   a gibbet-habitat
of poles and catheters   is home
to the bald woman who cannot
close her eyes at night
for looking

past it   past anything
TV's nightlong laugh riot
is not aware (how
could it be?) her
sleeplessness

may not outlast
the equinoctial
disturbances   the transitory
obbligato
of the snow

The New Yorker, March 14, 1994

POT NOMADS

Peripatetic, rooted nowhere really—
though lately mortgage-bound
to a plot of ground, a hideaway
in the conifers of the Berkshires,
a lilac bush by the mailbox
and, come April, a yardful, under
apple trees, of purple violets
I've not yet seen (will I
ever? half desperately
I sometimes wonder)—

for the nonce I'd been
tethered, between bus trips
here and there, to furnished
lodgings where the one thing
veritably flourishing
(I wasn't) was, on a coolly
sunny bedroom windowsill,
three potted primulas, royal-
blue corollas each engauded
yellow at the center,

brought by a kindly colleague
to cheer up the premises.
Left unwatered while I
gallivanted elsewhere,
they'd languish: the tough,
green, warty leaf-rosettes
would droop and then, repeatedly,
revive, put out new blooms,
bright nurslings of nothing but
the sun and more tap water.

Come March, when I travelled
to—hurray!—the Berkshires,
I took them with me, rashly
thinking there they might perhaps

be grounded. A two-foot snowfall
disposed of that. They wound up,
three potfuls of compacted rootlets,
stranded in hardnose Manhattan,
where yet again they showed
how tough they were.

Having missed the lilacs and
applebloom, the violets of April,
come June we belatedly put the
poor, sad, potbound nomads
into a flowerbed that now is
somehow ours; then, being
fickle as well as preoccupied,
forgot to think of them,
might not (who knows?) have
thought of them again, ever,

were it not that in October—windfalls
thick in the grass, a glory inhabiting
each of a thousand maples—a feeble
grubbing at late weeds uncovered
three stubborn leaf-rosettes, greenly
holding on. Hothouse origins behind
them, travels over, roofed under
by a thatch of mulch, a hood of snow,
out there, will they (I shiver, thinking)
make it through the winter?

The New Yorker, May 22, 1995

THE WINTER BIRD

Keeping cheerful—
id est, getting past another
winter solstice—well,

the streetwise local
mocker—soot-colored, spouseless,
tough, a treble triple

catcall, a beeped signal
from the shrubbery—has almost
done it, just as all

but the merest rueful
shrug came to seem pointless.
Mock on, mock on, droll

ornithological
Voltaire—your wit, as circumstances
shrink, is our survival.

The New Yorker, December 22, 1997

Notes by Amy Clampitt

All of the notes to follow were written by Clampitt herself for inclusion in the five books she published in her lifetime.

The Kingfisher

THE OUTER BAR (page 7)   An expedition to a bar island off the coast of Maine, as re-called in midwinter, is the occasion and the subject here. Of the particular island Louise Dickinson Rich wrote in *The Peninsula* (Chatham-Viking, 1958, 1971, p. 153): "When there's an unusually low run of tide it's possible to get over there by walking across the exposed sand bar to Inner Bar Island and then scrambling ankle-deep along a rocky reef to Outer Bar. But you can't stay very long. The minute the tide turns you have to start back. If you wait too long you're going to be stuck out there for twelve hours, or until the next low tide; that is, unless you can attract the attention of a pass-ing lobsterman who will take you off." Natural processes have lately made getting there a little easier, but not very much.

". . . fall, gall and gash the daylight": this phrase for the breaking surf derives, of course, from "The Windhover" by Gerard Manley Hopkins.

SEA MOUSE (page 8)   At the time of my sole encounter with the sea mouse—a glimpse of a swimming creature in a rock pool at low tide—I had no idea what in the world it could be. It was quickly identified by means of a pocket guide to seashore life. According to the *Columbia Encyclopedia*, it is a "marine worm of the genus *Aphrodite* with a short, broad, segmented body, found in moderately deep water. . . . The entire dorsal surface . . . is covered by long, feltlike threads called setae, which produce a brilliant iri-descence. . . . Sea mice commonly reach 6 to 8 inches in length and 2 inches in width. They are classified in the phylum Annelida, class Polychaeta, family Aphroditidae."

THE SUN UNDERFOOT AMONG THE SUNDEWS (page 13)   SUNDEW. Any of several in-sectivorous plants of the genus *Drosera*, growing in wet ground and having leaves cov-ered with sticky hairs.

—*American Heritage Dictionary*

299

A PROCESSION AT CANDLEMAS (page 15) Fernand Braudel, *The Mediterranean and the Mediterranean World in the Age of Philip II,* vol. I, translated by Siân Reynolds (Harper & Row, 1972, pp. 87, 88): "Transhumance . . . is simply one form of the Mediterranean pastoral way of life, alternating between the grazing lands of the plains and the mountain pastures. . . . Nomadism, on the contrary, involves the whole community and moves it long distances. . . . Today nomadism . . . consists of the knot of about ten people who might be seen round a fire at nightfall in one of the outer suburbs of Beirut; or at harvest time in Algeria, a few camels, sheep and donkeys, two or three horses, some women dressed in red, and a few black goat-skin tents amidst the stubble . . ."

Candlemas, celebrated on February 2, is the Christian feast of the Purification of the Virgin and the Presentation of the Infant Jesus in the Temple.

Peter Levi, text of *The Greek World,* photographs by Eliot Porter (Dutton, 1980, p. 77): "Archaeologists have pieced together in some detail the progress of the building on the Acropolis and have identified more than seventy-five different hands on the carving of the sculptures that made up the frieze of the Parthenon. Beginning in the southwest corner of the temple, it represented one of the city's greatest ceremonies, the Panathenaic procession that every four years brought a new sacred robe, the peplos, to Athena. Altogether the carvings showed more than four hundred human figures and more than two hundred animals. Undoubtedly that procession did, in real life, wind past the Parthenon. But the priest and priestess who stand among the gods are the servants of the ancient, doll-like wooden image of Athena, whose sanctuary had always been on the spot where the Erechtheum now stands. And it was to that wooden image—rather than to the monumental figure of Athena, made of marble, gold, and ivory, that was the central feature of the completed Parthenon—that the new robe was offered." Similar wooden images were central to the worship of Artemis at Brauron, and of Hera at Argos and Samos.

TIMES SQUARE WATER MUSIC (page 21) The Times Square subway station in New York City is, among other things, a transfer point between the Interborough Rapid Transit and the Brooklyn-Manhattan Transit lines—hence IR and BM T. The initials N, RR, and QB, on the other hand, refer to particular routes on the BMT line; so far as I know, they mean nothing in particular.

Spleenwort is a kind of fern, and ouzels and pipits are small birds, all associated with water.

THE KINGFISHER (page 29) The design here might be thought of as an illuminated manuscript in which all the handwork happens to be verbal, or (perhaps more precisely) as a novel trying to work itself into a piece of cloisonné. Its subject is an episodic love affair that begins in England and is taken up again in New York City. Dylan Thomas died there, at St. Vincent's Hospital, in November 1953.

The kingfisher described in the final stanza is the European species, *Alcedo atthis,* which is conspicuous for its iridescent blue-green plumage. It is associated with the story of Alcyone and Ceyx, whom, in Ovid's *Metamorphoses*, Zeus turned into a pair of birds, and with the idea of "halcyon days"—a period of calm seas, and of general peace and serenity.

BEETHOVEN, OPUS 111 (page 35)   Beethoven's piano sonata no. 32, Opus 111 (the arabic numbers tend to be misread and even, unfortunately, misprinted as a Roman numeral III, which would make it an early rather than a late composition) is his last work in that form, dating to the early 1820s. It figures in Thomas Mann's *Dr. Faustus* (Knopf, 1948; Vintage Books edition pp. 53–56), in E. M. Forster's *A Room with a View* (Knopf, 1932, p. 54), and in Milan Kundera's *The Book of Laughter and Forgetting* (Knopf, 1981, p. 161). I was first exposed to it, so far as I know, at a recital by Norman Carey, to whom the poem is dedicated. The notes by Eric Blom to the recording by Artur Schnabel on the Seraphim label have added much to my own understanding of the music.

Putti: the stylized infant cherubs that appear to soar, plunge, or hover in some Italian and Spanish paintings on Christian themes.

"Beethoven might declare the air / his domicile, the winds kin": in a letter to Count Brunswick dated February 13, 1814, Beethoven wrote: "As regards me, great heavens! my dominion is in the air; the tones whirl like the wind, and often there is a whirl in my soul." Quoted in *Beethoven: The Man and the Artist, as Revealed in His Own Words,* edited by Friedrich Kerst and H. E. Krehbiel (Dover, 1964).

THE WOODLOT (page 39)   Again according to the Iowa Guide, the anonymous inventor of barbed wire was an Iowa farmer.

IMAGO (page 41)   Imago. 1. An insect in its sexually mature adult stage after metamorphosis. 2. *Psychoanalysis.* An often idealized image of a person, usually a parent, formed in childhood and persisting into adulthood.   —*American Heritage Dictionary*

". . . the lit pavilions / that seduced her, their tailed child . . .": the reference is to Hans Christian Andersen's tale of the Little Mermaid, whose yearning to leave the water and become a human biped was fulfilled, but at a price. For reasons I can only guess at, this story affected me more powerfully than anything else I read as a child. Recently I have connected it—however fancifully—with the seas that in past eons covered the region where I grew up. From *Basin and Range,* by John McPhee (Farrar, Straus & Giroux, 1981): "Ohio, Indiana, Illinois, and so forth, the whole of what used to be called the Middle West, is shield rock covered with a sedimentary veneer that has never been metamorphosed, never been ground into tectonic hash—sandstones, siltstones, limestones, dolomites, flatter than the ground above them, the silent floors of departed oceans, of epicratonic seas. Iowa. Nebraska."

Pheromones: From Lewis Thomas, *The Lives of a Cell* (Viking, 1974, pp. 17–18):

"Most of the known pheromones are small, simple molecules, active in extremely small concentrations. . . . The messages are urgent, but they may arrive, for all we know, in a fragrance of ambiguity. 'At home, 4 p.m. today,' says the female moth, and releases a brief explosion of bombykol, a single molecule of which will tremble the hairs of any male within miles and send him driving upwind in a confusion of ardor."

PALM SUNDAY (page 45)   "Sing, my tongue, the glorious battle" is from a processional hymn, the *Pange Lingua,* for which the sixth-century priest Venantius Fortunatus (later canonized) supplied the opening lines; it is still sung at church services on Palm Sunday.

REMEMBERING GREECE (page 46)   From *Face of North America,* by Peter Farb (Harper & Row, 1963, pp. 20–21): "The myriad offshore islands on the Maine coast are the summits of hills drowned by the advance of the ocean upon the land. . . . In preglacial times some of the islands that now loom out of the ocean, such as Monhegan, must have been mountains that soared above the plain. . . . One obvious cause of the submergence of the shoreline is the melt of the glaciers. . . . But the immense weight of the glaciers themselves probably accounted for the major part of the submergence. . . . The land has since rebounded somewhat, but it is still about 1200 feet lower than at the beginning of the glacial age."

Aeschylus, *Agamemnon,* translated by Richmond Lattimore (*Complete Greek Tragedies,* vol. 1, Modern Library, p. 70):

> . . . My maidens there!
> Why this delay? Your task has been appointed you,
> to strew the ground before his feet with tapestries.
> Let there spring up into this house he never hoped
> to see, where Justice leads him in, a crimson path.

RAIN AT BELLAGIO (page 47)   The scheme may be clearer if this poem is thought of as a meditation in the form of a travelogue: the narrator, just arrived in Italy, is met at Naples by a friend who has been living with her father at a villa on Lake Como, and who is about to join an order of contemplative nuns in England.

Fernand Braudel, *The Mediterranean and the Mediterranean World in the Age of Philip II,* vol. I, translated by Siân Reynolds (Harper & Row, 1972, pp. 74, 76): "Rice growing in Lombardy meant the enslavement under terrible conditions of workers who were unable to voice any effective protest since they were not organized. Rice fields do not require labour all the year round, but large numbers of casual workers for a few weeks, at the times of sowing, transplanting, and harvest. This kind of agriculture depends entirely on seasonal migration. It hardly requires the landowner to be present except for paying wages and overseeing the gangs at work. . . .

"The vast low-lying plain of the Sienese Maremma, a real fever trap, is, like its neighbour the Tuscan Maremma, dotted with noblemen's castles. . . . Most of the year the masters live in Siena, in the huge town houses still standing today, palaces into which Bandello's lovers find their way, with the ritual complicity of the servants. . . . [The] dénouement would take place in secret in the old castle in the Maremma, far from the town gossip and family control. Isolated from the world by fever and the sultry heat, what better place could there be for putting to death, according to the custom of Italy and the century, of an unfaithful wife—or one suspected of being so?"

OR CONSIDER PROMETHEUS (page 56)   It was Daniel Gabriel, in a poetry workshop at The New School, who led me to Charles Olson's *Call Me Ishmael* (City Lights Books, 1947), as a book no American poet should fail to read. For this advice, along with much else, I here acknowledge my indebtedness.

"The smuggled gem / inside the weed stem": Prometheus is said to have carried fire down from Olympus inside the stalk of a giant fennel.

Whales, dolphins, and porpoises are all air-breathing mammals; even though they spend their entire lives in the water, they must rise to the surface periodically to replenish their supply of oxygen. It is presumed that they evolved from a land-dwelling ancestor, whose ancestor in turn was an ocean-dwelling fish. What prompted this return to a life in the oceans is a matter of speculation—and although volition has no place in any theory of evolution, strictly speaking, the notion of a Road Not Taken becomes almost irresistible when the habits of the ocean-dwelling mammals and those of the tree-dwelling, prehensile, visually oriented monkeys (whose habits our own so much resemble) are compared.

THE DAHLIA GARDENS (page 61)   An account of the self-immolation of a thirty-two-year-old Quaker, Norman Morrison, in front of the Pentagon in Washington appeared in *The New York Times* on November 3, 1965. Although his name has since been forgotten in the United States, in 1978 it was (according to an American visitor whose report I happened to hear) still remembered in Vietnam.

"Midway between Wilmington and Philadelphia": the refineries of Marcus Hook, Pennsylvania, with their perpetual gas flares, will be familiar to anyone who has traveled through the region via Amtrak.

Charles Olson's observation that the first oil well had been drilled as recently as 1859 was what dramatized for me the transitoriness of an entire culture founded on the use of petroleum: people to whom I report this fact are almost invariably startled, as though it could not possibly be true.

THE BURNING CHILD (page 67)   The account from which the epigraph is taken appears at the beginning of Chapter VII of *The Interpretation of Dreams*, "The Psychology of the Dream-Processes," and is quoted here from the translation by James Strachey (Avon, 1965, pp. 547–48).

What The Light Was Like

THE AUGUST DARKS (page 71)   "Herring prefer to come inshore on the dark of the moon," according to a report published in the *Ellsworth* [Maine] *American* for August 5, 1982, and headlined "The August Darks."

From *Middlemarch*, by George Eliot, Book II, Chapter 20: "If we had a keen vision and feeling of all ordinary human life, it would be like hearing the grass grow and the squirrel's heart beat, and we should die of that roar which lies on the other side of silence. As it is, the quickest of us walk about well wadded with stupidity."

LOW TIDE AT SCHOODIC (page 73)   From *The Geology of Acadia National Park* by Carleton A. Chapman (Chatham Press, 1970): "An outstanding feature of Schoodic Point is the abundance of dark-colored basaltic dikes, which range up to many yards in width and run through the granite ledges. . . . About 450 million years ago . . . the sea covered a large part of New England and widespread layers of sand, silt, and mud were accumulating upon its floor. . . . After these . . . had accumulated to a total thickness of hundreds and perhaps even thousands of feet, the southeastern portion of Maine became an unstable region and crustal movement (diastrophism) set in. . . . Hot fluid, similar to the black lava of Hawaii's volcanoes, was squeezed upward and sought the easiest means of access to the stratified rocks above. Zones of weakness, such as large fractures in the crustal rocks, permitted rapid influx of the magma. . . ."

From *The Audubon Society Field Guide to North American Seashore Creatures* by Norman A. Meinkoth (Alfred A. Knopf, 1981): "The white barnacles seen at low tide covering rocks and pilings on the seacoast are sedentary crustaceans. They secrete limy shells composed of many interlocking plates, often with a trapdoor opening at the top that can be closed for protection."

URN-BURIAL AND THE BUTTERFLY MIGRATION (page 90)   From *Hydriotaphia*, by Sir Thomas Browne, Chapter 1: "Time hath endless rarities, and shows of all varieties; which reveals old things in heaven, makes new discoveries in earth, and even earth it self a discovery. That great antiquity *America* lay buried for thousands of years; and a large part of the earth is still in the Urne unto us. . . . Many have taken voluminous pains to determine the state of the soul upon disunion; but men have been most phantasticall in the singular contrivances of their corporall dissolution: whilest the sobrest Nations have rested in two wayes, of simple inhumation and burning. . . . Some being of the opinion of *Thales*, that water was the originall of all things, thought it most equall to submit unto the principle of putrefaction, and conclude in a moist relentment. Others conceived it most natural to end in fire, as due unto the master principle in the composition, according to the doctrine of Heraclitus. . . . the old Heroes in *Homer* dreaded nothing more than water or drowning; probably upon the old opinion of the fiery substance of the soul. . . . " From Chapter 3 of the same work: "How the bulk of a man should sink into so few pounds of bones and ashes, may seem strange unto any who considers not its constitution, and how slender a masse will remain upon an open and urging fire of the carnall composition. Even bones themselves reduced into ashes, do abate a notable proportion. And consisting much of a volatile salt, when that is fired out, make a light kind of cinders. Although their bulk be disproportionable to their weight, when the heavy principle of Salt is fired out and the Earth almost only remaineth. . . . "

Monarch. . . . 4. a species of large, migrating butterfly of North America, having reddish-brown, black-edged wings: the larvae feed on milkweed.

—*Webster's New Universal Unabridged Dictionary*

VOYAGES: A HOMAGE TO JOHN KEATS (page 94) In the summer and early fall of 1816, John Keats spent two months at the seaside resort of Margate, on the English Channel. It was here that he saw the ocean for the first time. He was not quite twenty-one, and had only recently begun to think of himself as a poet. Not long after his return to London he stayed up all one night reading aloud with a friend from George Chapman's translation of the *Odyssey*, and wrote his now famous sonnet, "On First Looking into Chapman's Homer." In the spring of the following year he was back at Margate, reading Shakespeare and working on a long poem of his own. On May 10, 1817, he wrote to his friend B. R. Haydon, "I have been in such a state of Mind as to read over my Lines and hate them. I am 'one that gathers Samphire dreadful trade' the cliff of Poesy towers above me. . . ."—a reference to Act IV, Scene 6, of *King Lear*:

Come, sir; here is the place: stand still. How fearful
And dizzy 'tis to cast one's eyes so low!
The crows and choughs that wing the midway air
Show scarce so gross as beetles; half way down
Hangs one that gathers samphire, dreadful trade!

(Samphire or glasswort is a fleshy seaside herb that is at least better to eat than nothing.) In that scene Gloucester, who has been blinded for remaining loyal to King Lear, is being led through the countryside near Dover, which is not many miles down the coast from Margate itself—a circumstance that must have added to its effect on Keats's own imagination. The powerful way in which literature can become a link with times and places, and with minds, otherwise remote, suggested itself to me as I read W. Jackson Bate's biography, *John Keats* (Harvard University Press, 1963). It was here that I came upon the account by a contemporary, Joseph Severn, of how Keats would pause during a walk across Hampstead Heath to watch the passage of the wind over a field of grain: "The sea, or thought-compelling images of the sea, always seemed to restore him to a happy calm." The idea of John Keats pausing to take in a sight that had been familiar to me since childhood connected itself in turn with images of the ocean in the work of Whitman and Hart Crane. For connecting Keats with Osip Mandelstam, there is at any rate the authority of Nadezhda Mandelstam's observation (in *Mozart and Salieri*, p. 23): "Akhmatova used to say that Keats almost physiologically reminded her of Mandelstam." And that Wallace Stevens might also be intimately linked with Keats was suggested to me by an essay of Helen Vendler, "Stevens and Keats' 'To Autumn'" (in *Part of Nature, Part of Us*, Harvard University Press, 1980), for which I wish here to acknowledge my enormous indebtedness.

The lines quoted in the epigraph are from an untitled octet, as translated by David McDuff in *Osip Mandelstam: Selected Poems* (Farrar, Straus & Giroux, 1975; p. 129). Other poems paraphrased or alluded to in the concluding poem of the sequence may be found on pp. 11, 37, 111, 123, and 163 of the same volume.

In the final poem of the sequence, the third and fourth stanzas draw upon "Porphyro in Akron" from *The Complete Poems and Selected Letters and Prose of Hart Crane*, edited by Brom Weber (Anchor Books, New York, 1966, pp. 144–46), which concludes:

> But look up, Porphyro,—your toes
> Are ridiculously tapping
> The spindles at the foot of the bed.
>
> The stars are drowned in a slow rain,
> And a hash of noises is slung up from the street.
> You ought, really, to try to sleep,
> Even though, in this town, poetry's a
> Bedroom occupation.

THE REEDBEDS OF THE HACKENSACK (page 115)   Reed, n. . . . . 1. any of various tall, broad-leaved, related grasses with jointed, hollow stems which grow along the banks of streams . . . especially *Phragmites communis*, the common reed. This is the largest of all the grasses of northern climates, and one of the most universally diffused. It is used for thatching, for protecting embankments, for roofing, etc. 2. a mass of these, growing or dried. 3. a rustic musical instrument made from a hollow stem or stalk and played by blowing through it: used as the symbol of pastoral poetry.

—*Webster's New Universal Unabridged Dictionary*

From *Return to the Marshes: Life with the Marsh Arabs of Iraq* by Gavin Young (Collins, London, 1977, pp. 16, 34): ". . . often, out of some apparently deserted reed-jungle, a full-throated human voice soared into the silence—a young Marsh Arab singing a love-song as he harvested the rushes. . . . In that great solitude, where the men of Ur once poled their canoes and where 'in the beginning,' according to Sumerian legend, Marduk, the great God, built a reed platform on the surface of the waters and thus created the world, the effect is one of unquenchable and universal yearning. . . . The numerous Sumerian city-states . . . were large and sophisticated settlements consisting of suburbs, satellite towns, gardens and orchards. . . . In the cities on the fringe of the giant reed-beds, writing was born (about 3000 B.C.) and developed, at first in the form of pictographs, simple drawings scratched on clay with reed stalks. . . ."

Allusions to and/or borrowings from the poems of William Carlos Williams, Dante, Milton, Keats, and Shakespeare will be noted in this poem, which may be regarded as a last-ditch effort to associate the landscape familiarly known as the Jersey Meadows with the tradition of elegiac poetry.

REAL ESTATE (page 117) "Urban Relocation (Not A / Governmental Agency)": A private firm retained by the owners of tenement buildings intended for demolition but still inhabited, Urban Relocation had chosen a name of such bureaucratic portentousness that it was obliged to distinguish itself in this fashion.

HOMER, A.D. 1982 (page 119) The descriptive epithet πολνφλοίσβοιο-θαλάσσης (variously translated as "loud-roaring," "heavy-thundering," or simply "murmuring" and pronounced *poluphloísboio-thalássēs*) recurs throughout the *Iliad;* its first appearance is in line 34 of the first book, in which the reader sees "the spurned priest of Apollo shrink along the shore." The surprising eloquence of Odysseus is described in lines 216–23 of the third book, and the scene in which the infant Astyanax is frightened by the sight of his father Hector in the horsehair-plumed war helmet he wore as he said goodbye to his family occurs in Book 6, lines 466–70.

LOSING TRACK OF LANGUAGE (page 122) The Canzone of Petrarch referred to in the second stanza is the one beginning, "Chiare, fresche e dolci aque." The poem of Sappho referred to in the concluding stanza is Number 20 in *Sappho: A New Translation* by Mary Barnard (University of California Press, Berkeley and Los Angeles, 1958).

Archaic Figure

ARCHAIC FIGURE (page 127) From E. Homann-Wedeking, *The Art of Archaic Greece,* translated by J. R. Foster (Greystone Press, 1968, pp. 96–97, 98): "There [on the island of Samos], about 560 B.C., a donor erected in the sanctuary of Hera a long base on which six marble statues stood side by side. . . . All the figures had names inscribed on them. The artist, Geneleos by name, also inscribed his own name. . . . The execution of each individual figure is unsurpassable. The statue of Ornithe can serve as an example. The special delicacy of the surface texture lies in the quite shallow modelling and the tender, tranquil play of the folds of drapery. . . . The garment is brought to life by the quiet gesture of the right hand lightly catching up the material. Statues like that of Ornithe were the prototypes which inspired the sculptors of the other regions of Greece to produce similar works. The clothing alone would show that Ionia was the source of these figures. There the oldest of them are dressed in the chiton, a tunic-like garment made of thin, delicate material. . . ."

From Fernand Braudel, *The Mediterranean* (Harper & Row, 1975, vol. 1, p. 241): "The truth is that the Mediterranean has struggled against a fundamental poverty, aggravated but not entirely accounted for by circumstances. It affords a precarious living, in spite of its apparent or real advantages. It is easy to be deceived by its famous charm and beauty. Even as experienced a geographer as Philippson was dazzled, like all visitors from the North, by the sun, the colours, the warmth, the winter roses, the early fruits. Goethe at Vicenza was captivated by the popular street life with its open stalls and dreamed of taking back home with him a little of the magic air of the South. Even when one is aware of the reality it is difficult to associate these scenes of brilliance and gaiety with images of misery and physical hardship."

TEMPE IN THE RAIN (page 130)   From *New Larousse Encyclopedia of Mythology* (Prometheus Press, 1968, pp. 95–96): "The mariner who sailed into the gulf of Therme (today the gulf of Salonica) would feel himself filled with religious awe when he perceived against the hard blue line of sky the lofty profile of Mount Olympus. Everything concurred to reveal to him the fearful majesty of the gods. In the first place he had no doubt that Olympus was the highest mountain in the world. Then he would remember that the narrow Vale of Tempe, which separates Olympus from Ossa and cradles under its willows and plane-trees the peaceful stream of Peneus, had been hollowed out by Zeus during his struggle with the Titans."

THERMOPYLAE (page 132)   From Book Seven of the *Histories* of Herodotus, translated by Aubrey de Selincourt (Penguin Books, 1954, p. 493): "There was a bitter struggle over the body of Leonidas; four times the Greeks drove the enemy off, and at last by their valour succeeded in dragging it away. So it went on, until the fresh troops with Ephialtes were close at hand; and then, when the Greeks knew that they had come, the character of the fighting changed. They withdrew again into the narrow neck of the pass, behind the walls, and took up a position in a single compact body—all except the Thebans—on the little hill at the entrance to the pass, where the stone lion in memory of Leonidas stands today. Here they resisted to the last, with their swords, if they had them, and, if not, with their hands and teeth, until the Persians, coming on from the front over the ruins of the wall and closing in from behind, finally overwhelmed them."

LEAVING YÁNNINA (page 133)   Yánnina: a lakeside town in northern Greece. *Volta:* the evening promenade that is a custom in Mediterranean countries.

MEDUSA (page 134)   On the Gorgons, from *A Handbook of Greek Mythology*, by H. J. Rose (Dutton, 1959, pp. 29–30): "With regard to the Gorgons, it has been rightly pointed out, for instance by Miss Harrison, that we hear of the head of the Gorgon before anything is told us of the Gorgon herself. The kernel of the myth is, that there existed sometime and somewhere a creature of aspect so terrible that those who saw her turned at once into stone. . . . Once started on its way, this idea would naturally blend with the widespread superstition, common in both ancient and modern Greece, of the evil eye. . . . The older Greek art . . . shows a horrible, grinning head, with flat nose, lolling tongue, and staring eyes, sometimes adding a striding, winged body. With this the descriptions of poets later than Homer correspond. In particular several passages give the Gorgons serpents in their hair or girdles, with other monstrous features. . . . As a result of the Greek hatred of ugliness, or possibly to avoid representing Poseidon as being in love with anything so misshapen as the traditional Gorgon, later art shows Medusa as a beautiful woman, from about 300 B.C. on, with a look of terror or pain about the eyes."

HIPPOCRENE (page 138)   From *The Diary of Virginia Woolf,* edited by Anne Olivier Bell (Harcourt Brace Jovanovich, 1980, vol. 3, p. 113): "Thursday 30 September. I wished to add some remarks to this, on the mystical side of this solitude; how it is not oneself but something in the universe that one's left with. It is this that is frightening & exciting in the midst of my profound gloom, depression, boredom, whatever it is: One sees a fin passing far out. What image can I reach to convey what I mean? Really there is none I think. The interesting thing is that in all my feeling & thinking I have never come up against this before. Life is, soberly & accurately, the oddest affair; has in it the essence of reality. I used to feel this as a child—couldn't step across a puddle once I remember, for thinking, how strange—what am I? &c. But by writing I dont reach anything. All I mean to make is a note of a curious state of mind. I hazard the guess that it may be the impulse behind another book. . . ."

ATHENA (page 139)   **ae´gis, e´gis,** n. [L. from Gr. *aigis,* a goatskin, from *aix, aigos,* a goat.]
    1. in Greek mythology, a shield or breastplate; originally applied to the shield worn by Jupiter. In later times, a part of the armor of Pallas Athena, appearing as a kind of breastplate covered with metal scales and the head of the Gorgon Medusa, and fringed with serpents.

—Webster's Unabridged Dictionary

ATLAS IMMOBILIZED (page 141)   The story of how, after refusing hospitality to Perseus, the giant Atlas was transformed into a mountain, is told in the *Metamorphoses* of Ovid, Book IV.

HIGHGATE CEMETERY (page 145)   In a letter to Robert Bridges dated 28 October 1886, Gerard Manley Hopkins wrote: "How admirable are Blackmore and Hardy! Their merits are much eclipsed by the overdone reputation of the Evans-Eliot-Cross woman (poor creature! one ought not to speak slightingly, I know), half real power, half imposition. . . ." (*Selected Prose*, edited by Gerald Roberts, Oxford University Press, 1980, p. 148.)

GRASMERE (page 147)   Whatever may be conjectured about the attachment between Dorothy Wordsworth and her brother William—and there has been much conjecture, most recently by Robert Gittings and Jo Manton in *Dorothy Wordsworth* (Oxford, 1985)—the undisputed circumstances are that they were born a year apart, were separated at the age of seven and eight respectively and saw little of one another until they were in their teens; that once reunited, they lived together, with brief separations, from 1794 until William's death in 1850 (Dorothy, although for many years incapacitated, survived him by five years); that during a stay in France, William fell in love with Annette Vallon, by whom in 1792 he had a daughter, Caroline; and that in 1802 William married Dorothy's longtime friend Mary Hutchinson, by whom he had five more children—John, Dorothy, Thomas, Catharine, and William, Jr. From December 1799 until the spring of 1808, the Wordsworths made their home at Grasmere, in what is now known as Dove Cottage; here, at various times, Samuel Taylor Coleridge, and later Thomas De Quincey, were part of the household. In 1813, after living briefly at two other houses in Grasmere itself, the family moved to Rydal Mount, where Dorothy, William, and Mary would all reside for the rest of their lives.

COLEORTON (page 151)   "Wordsworth . . . has been described," wrote Douglas Bush in *Mythology and the Romantic Tradition in English Poetry* (Harvard University Press, 1969, p. 51), "as Coleridge's greatest work, and, like all his other works, left unfinished."

From the letters of Dorothy Wordsworth, as quoted in Gittings and Manton, pp. 155ff.: "We are crammed in our little nest edge full as you will suppose. . . . Every bed lodges two persons at present." (January 1806) "Our continuing here during another winter would be attended with so many serious inconveniences, especially to my Brother, who has no quiet corner in which to pursue his studies, no room but that where we all sit (to say nothing of the unwholesomeness of these low small rooms for such a number of persons). . . . We think of going into Leicestershire, Sir George B[eaumont] having offered us their house for the winter." (June 1806)

AN ANATOMY OF MIGRAINE (page 157)   From Thomas De Quincey, *Confessions of an English Opium-Eater* (Oxford University Press, 1985, p. 76): "The dream commenced with a music which now I often heard in dreams—a music of preparation and of awakening suspense; a music like the opening of the Coronation Anthem, and which, like *that*, gave the feeling of a vast march—of infinite cavalcades filing off—and the tread of innumerable armies."

From Simone Weil, *Gravity and Grace* (G. P. Putnam's Sons, 1952, pp. 7, 73–74): "Nothing in the world can rob us of the power to say 'I.' Nothing except extreme affliction. Nothing is worse than extreme affliction which destroys the 'I' from outside, because after that we can no longer destroy it ourselves. What happens to those whose

'I' has been destroyed from outside by affliction? It is not possible to imagine anything for them but annihilation according to the atheistic or materialistic conception.

"Though they may have lost their 'I,' it does not mean that they have no more egoism. Quite the reverse. . . . Human injustice as a general rule produces not martyrs but quasi-damned souls. Beings who have fallen into this quasi-hell are like someone stripped and wounded by robbers. They have lost the clothing of character."

From Henry James, *The Wings of the Dove*, Book First (Modern Library Edition, 1930, pp. 36, 37): ". . . all intercourse with her sister had the effect of casting down her courage and tying her hands, adding daily to her sense of the part, not always either uplifting or sweetening, that the bond of blood might play in one's life. . . . Bereaved, disappointed, demoralized, querulous, she was all the more sharply and insistently Kate's elder and Kate's own. . . . She [Kate] noticed with profundity that disappointment made people selfish. . . ."

From *The Brain: Mystery of Matter and Mind* (U.S. News Books, 1981, p. 23): "Brain surgeon Roger Sperry of the California Institute of Technology concluded that the brain's consciousness encompassed and transcended its physical workings: 'In the human head there are forces within forces within forces, as in no other cubic half-foot of the universe that we know.' "

Again, from Simone Weil in *Gravity and Grace*, p. 133: "Time bears the thinking being in spite of himself toward that which he cannot bear, and which will come all the same."

From a note by Martin Gardner to *The Annotated Alice* (Bramhall House, 1960, p. 231): "Tweedledum and Tweedledee are what geometers call 'enantiomorphs,' mirror-image forms of each other. That Carroll intended this is strongly suggested by Tweedledee's favorite word, 'contrariwise,' and by the fact that they extend right and left hands for a handshake. Tenniel's picture of the two enantiomorphs arrayed for battle, standing in identical postures, indicates that he looked upon the twins in the same way. . . ."

chī-as′ma, n.; pl. **chī-as′mà-tà.** [Gr. *chiasma*, two lines crossed, from *chiazein*, to mark with the Greek letter chi.]

1. in anatomy, a crossing or intersection of the optic nerves on the ventral surface of the brain.

2. any crosswise fusion.

chī-as′mus, n.; pl. chī-as′mi. [Mod. L.: Gr. *chiasmos*, placing crosswise.] an inversion of the second of two parallel phrases, clauses, etc.; as, do not live to eat, but eat to live.

—Webster's Unabridged Dictionary

From *The Diary of Virginia Woolf,* edited by Anne Olivier Bell (Harcourt Brace Jovanovich, 1977–84): ". . . Often down here I have entered into a sanctuary; a nunnery; had a religious retreat; of great agony once; & always some terror: so afraid one is of loneliness: of seeing to the bottom of the vessel. That is one of the experiences I have had here in some Augusts; & got then to a consciousness of what I call 'reality': a thing I see before me, something abstract; but residing in the downs or sky; beside which nothing matters; in which I shall rest & continue to exist. Reality I call it. And I fancy sometimes this is the most necessary thing to me: that which I seek. But who knows—once one takes a pen & writes? . . ." (Monday 10 September 1928; vol. 3, p. 196.)

"I've had some very curious visions in this room too, lying in bed, mad, & seeing the sunlight quivering like gold water, on the wall. I've heard the voices of the dead here. And felt, through it all, exquisitely happy." (Wednesday 9 January 1924; vol. 2, p. 283.)

MAN FEEDING PIGEONS (page 174)   From the *Paradiso* of Dante Alighieri, Canto XXX:

> E se l'infimo grado in sè raccoglie
>   sì grande lume, quant' è la larghezza
>   di questo rosa nell' estreme foglie?

> (And if the lowest step gathereth so large
>   a light within itself, what then the amplitude
>   of the rose's outmost petals?)
>   —TRANSLATION BY PHILIP H. WICKSTEED

Westward

HAVING LUNCH AT BRASENOSE (page 192)   On Oxford, from *The Blue Guide to England* (Benn, 1980, pp. 274–75): "On the w. side of Radcliff Sq. is Brasenose College, founded in 1509 by Wm. Smyth, Bp. of Lincoln, and Sir Richard Sutton. The name is probably derived from the brazen knocker (a lion's head) of an older Hall, which was carried off to Stamford in 1334; this was recovered in 1890 and is kept in the college hall. Another derivation is from a supposed 'brasenhus' or brewery, on the site of the college."

WESTWARD (page 194)   From *Civilisation: A Personal View*, by Kenneth Clark (Harper & Row, 1969), p. 10:
"Iona was founded by St Columba, who came here from Ireland in the year 543. It seems to have been a sacred spot before he came and for four centuries it was the centre of Celtic Christianity. There are said to have been three hundred and sixty large stone crosses on the island, nearly all of which were thrown into the sea during the Reformation."

AMHERST (page 208)   The profile of Norwottuck, a low hill south of the town of Amherst that would have been familiar to Emily Dickinson, may be viewed from a site, new since her day, honoring graduates of Amherst College who served in the two world wars. The poet's death on May 15, 1886, has been commemorated in recent years by a gathering in the cemetery where she is buried.

Phrases lifted from the poems of Emily Dickinson will be evident. The ones represented include (using the numbers in *The Complete Poems of Emily Dickinson*, edited by Thomas H. Johnson) 526, 530, 663, 595, 658, 594, 601, 564, 593, 486. The most unlikely of these is the poet's reference (in poem 564) to "Vast Prairies of Air/Unbroken by a Settler." Her work is, however, studded with allusions to places she had never seen.

EASEDALE TARN (page 210)   From Thomas De Quincey, *Recollections of the Lakes and the Lake Poets* (Penguin, 1985, pp. 250–51): ". . . But there is a third advantage possessed by this Easedale, above other rival valleys, in the sublimity of its mountain barriers. In one of its many rocky recesses is seen a 'force,' (such is the local name for a cataract), white with foam, descending at all seasons with respectable strength, and, after the melting of snows, with an Alpine violence. Follow the leading of this 'force' for three quarters of a mile, and you come to a little mountain lake, locally termed a 'tarn,' the very finest and most gloomily sublime of its class."

MY COUSIN MURIEL (page 215)   The needlepoint lace known as *punto in aria*—literally, "a stitch in the air"—originated in Venice, according to the *Columbia Encyclopedia*, as laceworkers ventured beyond purely geometric designs on a ground of netting to freer ones with no ground at all.

Concerning Charles Wadsworth, from *The Life of Emily Dickinson* by Richard B. Sewall (Farrar, Straus & Giroux, 1980, pp. 449–50): "His popularity in Philadelphia has been compared with Henry Ward Beecher's in Brooklyn and his preaching was ranked second only to Beecher's in the country. In April 1862, he accepted a call from the Calvary Presbyterian Society in San Francisco . . . a move which was long thought . . . to account for Emily's complaint . . . of her 'terror since September . . .' In a letter to [Thomas Wentworth] Higginson a few months after Wadsworth died, he was 'my closest earthly friend.' "

NOTHING STAYS PUT (page 219)   The alstroemeria, like the freesia, is a cultivated flower named presumably for the botanist who first identified or classified it.

THE PRAIRIE (page 221)   Aside from the works of Chekhov and of Emerson quoted in the text, the sources drawn upon here include the privately printed *Some Incidents in My Life: A Saga of the "Unknown" Citizen*, by Frank T. Clampitt; *Iowa: A Bicentennial History*, by Joseph F. Wall (W. W. Norton, 1978); *The Book of the Omaha*, edited by Paul A.

Olson (Nebraska Curriculum Development Center, 1979); and *Pasadena: Crown of the Valley* (Windsor Publications, 1986).

The phrase quoted from George Eliot occurs in *Middlemarch*, Book II, Chapter 20.

Simone Weil wrote in her commentary entitled "The *Iliad;* or The Poem of Force": "Far from hot baths he was indeed, poor man. And not he alone. Nearly all the *Iliad* takes place far from hot baths. Nearly all of human life, then and now, takes place far from hot baths."

The descriptive phrase transliterated here as *poluphloisboio thalassēs* occurs for the first time near the beginning of the *Iliad*. It has been variously handled by translators— from "murmuring" to "loud-roaring" seas and back again. Tennyson perhaps had it in mind when he had his Ulysses say "the deep / Moans round with many voices." Nothing in English, however, comes so close as the Greek to the hissing and tumultuous force of the breaking waves themselves.

A Silence Opens

SYRINX (page 241)   "Then there gathered from out of Erebus the spirits of those that are dead, brides, and unwedded youths, and toil-worn old men, and tender maidens with hearts yet new to sorrow, and many, too, that had been wounded with bronze-tipped spears, men slain in fight, wearing their blood-stained armour. These came thronging in crowds about the pit from every side, with a wondrous cry. . . ." —*Odyssey*, vol. 1, XI:34–43, translated by A. T. Murray (William Heinemann Ltd., 1919).

HISPANIOLA (page 243)   "Right from the start, Columbus had a plan: to establish a sugar industry on Hispaniola much like the ones back on the Canary and Madeira islands. . . ." —Susan Miller, "Slavery: The High Price of Sugar," *Newsweek*, Special Issue, Fall/Winter 1991.

PAUMANOK (page 245)
> I too Paumanok, . . .
> I too leave little wrecks upon you, you fish-shaped island.
> —WALT WHITMAN, "As I Ebb'd with the Ocean of Life"

MATOAKA (page 247)   The sources drawn upon here include *Their Majesties' Royall College: William and Mary in the Seventeenth and Eighteenth Centuries*, by J. E. Morpurgo (1976); *Narratives of Early Virginia*, edited by Lyon Gardiner Tyler (1907); *Pocahontas*, by Grace Steele Woodward (1969); *The Virginia Guide* (1940, 1941); and *Undreamed Shores: England's Wasted Empire in America*, by Michael Foss (1974). The lines by Sir Walter Raleigh are from "His Epitaph"; those by Michael Drayton, from "To the Virginian Voyage."

SHOREBIRD-WATCHING (page 256) The Althing is the parliament of Iceland. "Thingstead" is the name given to the meeting place of such a body.

'EIGHTY-NINE (page 269)

> . . . Not that you could bear
> the voice of God—far from it. But hear the wind's blowing,
> the uninterrupted tidings created from silence,
> they sweep toward you now from those who died young.
>
> Every angel is terrible. And yet, alas,
> I welcome you, almost fatal birds of the soul. . . .
>
> —RAINER MARIA RILKE, *Duino Elegies*,
> TRANSLATED BY C. F. MACINTYRE

SED DE CORRER (page 276) *The Complete Posthumous Poetry* of César Vallejo, translated by Clayton Eshleman and José Rubia Barcia (1978), is the source of the passages quoted here. *Poet in New York*, by Federico García Lorca, translated by Greg Simon and Steven F. White (1988), has been similarly drawn upon. I am indebted to Cecilia Vicuña for particular help and inspiration.

MATRIX (page 281) "The Madonna of Montserrato is one of the most revered Madonnas of Spain, before whose statue in the abbey of Montserrato St. Ignatius Loyola laid down his sword and dagger to become a warrior of the church. . . . The oil painting of the Madonna that graces the present 19th-century chapel, by style clearly of the late 16th century and hence an altar piece in the original church [built at Bellagio by Ercole Sfondrati in the year 1591], portrays a Madonna holding the Child . . . wielding a saw like those still seen in Bellagio, a small 'buck-saw,' and he is using it to cut saw teeth into the mountains in the background. Perhaps the implication is that the Child sawed off the great slab of limestone on which the Bellagio chapel stands. Have we here a kind of baroque pun? It is a fact that in the Spanish Montserrato there is a dim tradition that its saw-toothed mountains were shaped by angels wielding golden saws." —*The Castle's Keep: The Villa Serbelloni in History*, by John Marshall (1970, p. 101).

A SILENCE (page 285) ". . . while walking one day in Boston, he saw the streets suddenly shrink and divide. His everyday preoccupations, his past, all the claims of the future fell away and he was enfolded in a great silence. . . . At the age of twenty-one [T. S.] Eliot had one of those experiences which, he said, many have had once or twice in their lives and been unable to put into words." —*Eliot's Early Years*, by Lyndall Gordon (1977, p. 15).
    ". . . dignity and majesty have I seen but once, as it stood in chains at midnight in

a dungeon in an obscure village in Missouri." —Letter written by Parley Pratt on Joseph Smith in jail, quoted by Fawn Brodie in *No Man Knows My History: The Life of Joseph Smith* (1986, p. 243).

". . . also I saw the infinite love of God, and I had great openings." —*The Journal of George Fox.*

Short Chronology

1920 Born at Cedardale Farm near New Providence, Iowa, on June 15. First child to farmers, Roy Clampitt (1888–1973), a sometime school principal, and Pauline Felt Clampitt (1891–1979), a former home economics teacher. Their village of 200 was a community settled by Quakers. The family regularly attended the local Quaker meetinghouse—Honey Creek Friends Church— and the faith had profound significance for Clampitt, although she was to become a devout Episcopalian and would later leave all churchgoing: near the end of her life she said, "Whatever dogmatic certitude I had then has pretty much evaporated." Some in the family had literary inclinations. Roy privately printed an autobiography, *A Life I Did Not Plan,* in 1966, following the practice of his own father, Frank Clampitt, who printed a memoir in 1936, *Some Incidents in My Life: A Saga of the "Unknown" Citizen.* Amy's siblings were Lawrence (b. 1923), Richard (1925–1981), Beth (1928–1994), and Philip (b. 1930).

1926 Enrolled at New Providence Consolidated School, where she would be a student for all twelve grades.

1930 Moved with her family to Pioneer Farm, three miles from her first home. Rather than continue to work Roy's father's land, the Clampitts had a go at owning their own farm. Amy never entirely recovered from this "expulsion," which many poems, most directly "Black Buttercups," address. The family's life in the 1930s was laborious; a piano and good books kept culture alive in the home. Amy read aloud to her siblings by the fire, and wrote her own first poem at about the age of nine, though she later said her earliest ambition was to become a painter. A sonnet sequence that she wrote at sixteen survives. Amy had pen pals around the world, including two girls growing up in Germany during Hitler's rise to power. Amy, Beth, and Lawrence had all been named after characters in their mother's favorite book, *Little Women*, and Amy's own early favorite, *Alice's Adventures in Wonderland*, remained at the core of her imagination.

1941 Graduated Phi Beta Kappa from Grinnell College, where she was a staff member of the college literary magazine, *Tanager*, which also published her fiction. Moved to New York City and began graduate school in English literature at Columbia University, but dropped out almost immediately. A biographical note to her 1981 chapbook, *The Isthmus*, claims, "She headed for New York mainly, as she recalls, because she wanted to work in publishing and to live near the ocean." She would see herself as a New Yorker for her entire adult life.

1943 Found employment as a secretary at Oxford University Press, and eventually became promotions director for college textbooks. Forged some lasting friendships throughout the forties, notably with editor Phoebe Hoss, to whom she would dedicate "Manhattan: An Elegy" (later "Manhattan"), a major poem drafted in the 1980s and not published until 1991. Made and broke off an engagement, and became involved in several painful love affairs about which she later spoke and wrote guardedly. In World War II her brother Lawrence served in the Navy, while her brother Richard shared their parents' pacifist convictions: he was a conscientious objector.

1944 Visited Mexico for about two weeks, to join her parents, who were working in a Quaker public-service project. With her youngest brother, Philip, she traveled from Mexico City to Xochimilco and back.

1949 Traveled to England as first-prize winner in an essay contest sponsored by Oxford University Press. Visiting people connected to the press in several cities, she made friendships and kept an extraordinarily detailed journal of literary verve and polish. The immersion in the past, which this first trip across the Atlantic afforded her, "changed my life forever," she later wrote.

1950 Clampitt's sister, Beth, always considered both brilliant and odd, had a nervous breakdown and was diagnosed as schizophrenic. She was hospitalized, given shock treatments, and eventually underwent a prefrontal lobotomy.

1951 Left her position at Oxford University Press to travel in Europe for five months, and to write fiction. Her travel journals again consisted of voluminous, acutely observed narratives.

1952 Began work as a reference librarian for the National Audubon Society, deepening a lifelong fascination with birds; also began writing book reviews for *Audubon Magazine*. Her letters mentioned novel writing. It remains unclear what relation her surviving novel drafts of the 1950s and 1960s have to each other. In an interview published in *The Paris Review* in 1993, conducted by Robert E. Hosmer, Jr., Clampitt would say, "I wrote three novels. I can hardly remember them. I don't have any wish to think about them now. I didn't know how to write a novel. . . . They had to do with memories of my childhood."

1955 Befriended two painters, Peter Marcasiano and Mary Russel. Traveling to Europe, Clampitt revisited a number of cities she had seen in 1949.

1956 Wrote to her brother Philip, "I feel as if I could write a whole history of English literature, and know just where to place everybody in it, with hardly any trouble at all. The reason being, apparently, that I feel *I am in it.*" In spite of this confidence, she had failed to place any of her fiction, and had instructed her agent to stop sending a novel manuscript out to publishers. While visiting The Cloisters in New York City, she underwent a joyful spiritual awakening, which coincided with the composition of a long poem, "The Sun on the Stone." Later that year, "joining the [Episcopal] church became an absolute necessity," she wrote.

1959 Resigned from the Audubon Society, turning down a promotion: a spiritually weighty decision for which she consulted an Episcopal priest.

1960 Moved to Des Moines, where Beth was living, hoping to take care of her in their own apartment. The experiment lasted for some months, until a doctor advised against continuing. During this time, Clampitt worked on a novel. She returned to New York and stayed a week with the Sisters of St. John the Baptist at their home convent in New Jersey. This was the period in which Clampitt herself considered becoming a nun. She turned to work as a freelance editor and researcher, which she continued until 1977. She traveled to the Rockefeller Foundation's Bellagio Center at Villa Serbelloni, in Italy, with her friend Anne Marshall, soon to join a convent. (Marshall became Sister Mary John, a Benedictine nun and later an abbess in Kent, England, with whom Amy remained close by correspondence until her own death. Clampitt's 1982 poem "Rain at Bellagio" was dedicated to their mutual friend Doris Thompson Myers. Clampitt's journals of the early 1960s often included nearly daily devotional meditations.

1961 Began her involvement with West Village housing politics, protesting large-scale developments, poor housing conditions, and the neighborhood's loss of rented apartments to condominium conversions.

1962 With Doris Thompson (soon Myers) and her fiancé, took a camping trip west, from Des Moines to Berkeley.

1965 Traveled to Greece for the first time. Unpublished travel writing—about Greece and England, and a book-length manuscript of essays, *Gargoyles, Campaniles, and Clichés*—were written around this period.

1966 Reported to a friend that she had completed a novel for which a publisher was considering the first chapters.

1967 An increasing involvement in Vietnam War protests, from the mid-sixties onward, seen by some members of her family as her "dark period." She was, by her own account, made extremely upset and nervous by the war. Her abandonment this time of the writing of fiction took a political hue: "Novels, they're for peacetime," she told her nephew David Clampitt, "when people have time on their hands."

1968   Met Harold Korn (1929–2001). "Hal," then a professor of law at New York University, later and for many years at Columbia University, encountered her at a gathering for supporters of Senator Eugene McCarthy's presidential campaign. The romance began in earnest very quickly. Hal was nine years younger than Amy, and divorced; at the age of twenty-eight, he had been involved in a car accident with his first wife, both of whom were badly burned. Even after plastic surgery, he was to remain noticeably disfigured. At the time he met Clampitt, Korn was beginning to earn renown as a scholar in the field of conflicts of law. By Christmas she wrote that she was "on the greatest poetry-writing binge in my history . . . I never felt more alive."

1970–71   More intense political involvement: fund-raising for the Black Panthers; supporting the California grape boycott, the New York City squatters' movement, and John Lindsay's campaign for mayor; serving as secretary of Village Independent Democrats. She was arrested with a group of squatters moving into a vacant building; a second arrest led to a night in jail. Demonstrating in Washington against the Vietnam War, Clampitt picketed with the sign "Poet," identifying herself publicly as such for the first time. In this period, she met Bishop Paul Moore and demanded that the Episcopal Church make a stand against the war. Although Bishop Moore had himself led a peace mission to South Vietnam in 1970, Clampitt found his answer unsatisfactory, and told friends at the time that this was why she was leaving the church. In her 1990 essay "The Long, Long Wait: The Epistles to the Thessalonians," she gave another reason for leaving the church: "The trouble, above all, was its callousness toward the Jews."

1973   Amy moved into Hal's home at 165 East Sixty-fifth Street, apartment 4F, her primary residence until her death. She continued to rent her small apartment in Greenwich Village (354 West Twelfth Street), and kept it as her address for correspondence until 1979. Amy did not marry Hal until her last days, but their shared life had all the features of marriage. Friends roundly credited Hal for encouraging Amy to resume writing poems and submitting them for publication. *The New York Times* published her poem "The Existential Choice," and Washington Street Press published her first poetry chapbook, *Multitudes, Multitudes.* Her father died.

1974   Began taking nearly annual summer vacations with Hal in Corea, Maine, which she would call her favorite place to write. They were often joined by a few close friends and by Hal's mother.

1977 Took her first poetry workshop, at The New School, taught by the poet Daniel Gabriel; with the class assembled in a bar, she gave her first poetry reading. Began freelance editing work for E. P. Dutton.

1978 Clampitt's boss and mentor at Dutton, John (Jack) Macrae, passed some of Clampitt's poems to Howard Moss, poetry editor of *The New Yorker*. Moss began to approve her poems for publication (the first was "The Sun Underfoot Among the Sundews"), and he became a friend; by his death in 1987 he had accepted more than thirty of her poems. In her lifetime, Clampitt published forty-eight poems in the magazine; two more, "Pot Nomads" and "The Winter Bird," appeared posthumously. Her reputation remains firmly allied with *The New Yorker*.

1979 Mother died. Clampitt submitted poems to Peter Davison, poetry editor of *The Atlantic;* the manuscripts were read first by staff editor Mary Jo Salter. Salter wrote a fan letter to Clampitt, whose response initiated a literary correspondence and friendship.

1980–82 Published poems more widely in journals. Her first book, offered under several titles, was rejected by a number of publishers, including Atlantic Monthly Press and Scribner. Became mired in a years-long dispute with her landlord; fought eviction from her rent-controlled West Village apartment in order to prevent the building from being converted to co-op; eventually she was indeed evicted.

1981 A limited-edition poetry chapbook, *The Isthmus,* appeared from Coalition of Publishers for Employment. None of the poems in this chapbook or in its predecessor, *Multitudes, Multitudes,* was to appear in any of her later collections for Knopf. She began studying classical Greek at The New School. Her brother Richard died.

1982 Manuscript of *The Kingfisher,* as her poetry collection was now called, accepted by Alice Quinn for the Knopf Poetry Series. Clampitt took a second course in classical Greek, this time at Hunter College, that would further contribute to the ancient and modern Greek subject matter of many of her poems in the next years. She was awarded a Guggenheim Fellowship, and another from the Academy of American Poets. Left employment with E. P. Dutton. Traveled widely, mostly to give poetry readings, although she avoided airplanes and did not drive. Buses and trains, which appear often in her work, were her preferred modes of transportation.

1983 Her first trade collection of poems, *The Kingfisher,* dedicated to Hal, was published to great acclaim, including a four-page review in *The New York Review of Books* in which Helen Vendler wrote that the volume a hundred years from now would "have taken on . . . the documentary value of what, in the twentieth century, made up the stuff of culture." Clampitt was accepted almost immediately into the literary establishment not as a brilliant beginner but as a master. Gratified by the late attention, she was also profoundly confused, even depressed, by it. She traveled constantly to give readings, and with Hal took a long trip to England and Europe. Their stops included the Lake District, Kent, Venice, Yugoslavia, and Greece.

1984 Awarded an Honorary Doctorate by her alma mater, Grinnell College, and a Fellowship by the American Academy and Institute of Arts and Letters. Sarabande Press published a limited fine edition of the poem sequence "Voyages: A Homage to John Keats," dedicated to Helen Vendler; the poems would reappear in *What the Light Was Like*. Was awarded a residency from the Djerassi Program, Woodside, California. Her many readings included one at The Library of Congress. Accepted a position for 1984–85 as Writer-in-Residence at the College of William and Mary.

1985 Extensive travels. Read in London to The Poetry Society; judged the Arvon International Poetry Competition with Craig Raine and Anne Stevenson. Other English travels in Chichester and Yorkshire; she stopped in the French Alps and Berlin. *What the Light Was Like,* her second book of poems, was published by Knopf; Amy dedicated it to the memory of her brother Richard.

1986 Residency at Yaddo, where she read Wordsworth and his circle. Traveled, and stopped as usual that summer in Corea, Maine, before becoming Visiting Writer at Amherst College for 1986–87.

1987 *Archaic Figure,* her third book of poems, published by Knopf. It is dedicated to Howard Moss, Mary Jo Salter, and Peter Kybart, an actor and close friend in New York, originally from Germany, with whom she had traveled to Germany and Greece. Delivered "The Prairie," her longest work in verse, as the Phi Beta Kappa poem at Harvard University. Named a Member of the American Academy of Arts and Letters. Wrote first draft of a play. Howard Moss died; Alice Quinn became poetry editor of *The New Yorker;* Ann Close, who had recommended *The Kingfisher* to Quinn in 1982, became Clampitt's editor at Knopf.

1988 Ecco Press published her edition of *The Essential Donne*. More travels, including England. Served as Fannie Hurst Visiting Professor, Washington University of St. Louis. Gave presentations in both St. Louis and Cambridge, Massachusetts, as part of T. S. Eliot centennial celebrations.

1989 The Poets' Theatre presented a staged reading at the Lyric Stage in Boston of her play, *The Three of Us* (which had also been called *A Guilty Thing Surprised* and later became *Mad with Joy*), about the Wordsworths and Samuel T. Coleridge. Clampitt chosen as a Literary Lion by The New York Public Library. Began having troubles with vertigo, which persisted.

1990 *Westward,* her fourth collection of poems, dedicated to the memory of her parents and grandparents, published by Knopf. It included poems that first appeared that year in *Manhattan: An Elegy, and Other Poems,* with woodcuts by

Margaret Sunday, by University of Iowa Center for the Book. Named a chancellor of the Academy of American Poets.

1991 *Predecessors, Et Cetera: Essays* published by University of Michigan Press. Many of her touchstone authors considered, if briefly: among them the Wordsworths, Emily Dickinson, Henry James, and Marianne Moore. Returned to Italy as a Rockefeller Fellow at the Bellagio Center (scene of her 1982 poem "Rain at Bellagio," about her visit with Anne Marshall in 1960); she produced new poems there, such as "Matrix." In December, served as Elizabeth Drew Professor at Smith College.

1992 Worked for a month as a Master Artist at the Atlantic Center for the Arts in Florida. Asked by the College of William and Mary, where she had taught in 1984–85, to deliver an original poem in celebration of its three-hundredth anniversary. The college, concerned about the political implications of her reading aloud her long poem, "Matoaka" (a meditation on Pocahontas and John Smith), requested that she offer it on another occasion, and Clampitt withdrew the poem altogether. Received honorary degree from Bowdoin College. Named a MacArthur Prize Fellow. With Hal, she bought the first home of her life, in Lenox, Massachusetts. Karen Chase, a poet she befriended at Bellagio in 1991, had a permanent home in Lenox (a town associated, too, with one of Clampitt's favorite "predecessors," Edith Wharton).

1993 Returned to Smith College in the spring, when she was named the first Grace Hazard Conkling Writer-in-Residence. In April, she learned she had ovarian cancer. Underwent surgery. Published essay "Lasting Through the Night," in *Where We Stand: Women Poets on Literary Tradition.* The journal *Verse* published an issue in Clampitt's honor, with an interview and poems, and essays by seven critics. The Lenox house, bought as a weekend and summer retreat, became her primary home, except when she was in New York for chemotherapy treatments.

1994 Her final book, *A Silence Opens,* dedicated to the memory of Marjorie Bates Pratt, a Maine poet friend, published by Knopf in February. A translation of Canto 9 of Dante's *Inferno* was included. Her essay "The Poetry of Isaiah" published in *Out of the Garden: Women Writers on the Bible.* Though very ill, in April she took a trip with Karen Chase to Key West, Florida, a place she had always wanted to see; she had further surgery in May. She and Hal were married, by a justice of the peace, in their home in Lenox, on June 2, attended by three witnesses. She died at the Lenox house on September 10. At a service held there several days later, her ashes were buried in the backyard. Her sister Beth died in November. In December, a public memorial service was held for Amy at the Cathedral of St. John the Divine, New York.

1997 *The Collected Poems of Amy Clampitt* published by Knopf, with a foreword by Mary Jo Salter.

2001 Harold Korn died. He had recently established the Amy Clampitt Fund, for the promotion of poetry and Clampitt's legacy. He left instructions for the Lenox house's regular use by a Clampitt Fellow: a poetry critic, or poet, in residence.

2003 Willard Spiegelman became the first Clampitt Fellow.

2005 *Love, Amy: The Selected Letters of Amy Clampitt*, edited by Spiegelman, published by Columbia University Press.

2010 Now in its seventh year, the Clampitt house has hosted, so far, eleven poets and critics, for six to twelve months each.

Suggestions for Further Reading

Essays by Amy Clampitt

"Providence." [citation to follow]

"The Poetry of Isaiah." *Out of the Garden: Women Writers and the Bible.* Ed. Celina Spiegel and Christina Buchmann. New York: Fawcett Columbine, 1994.

"Lasting Through the Night." *Where We Stand: Women Poets on Literary Tradition.* Ed. Sharon Bryan. New York: W. W. Norton and Company, 1993.

Essays about Amy Clampitt

No biography of Amy Clampitt, or full-length critical study of her work, has yet appeared.

The website amyclampitt.org reproduces with permission all of the essays published in Amy Clampitt's honor in the Special Issue of the journal *Verse* (10: 3, 1993). Some of these essays were later published in book form by the critics:

Costello, Bonnie. "Amy Clampitt: Nomad Exquisite."

Goodridge, Celeste. "Theatricality and Interiority: Amy Clampitt's Performances."

Jordan, Barbara. "Vision as Appetite: Clampitt as Naturalist."

Ramazani, Jahan. "'Nucleus of Fire': Amy Clampitt's Elegies for Her Parents."

Seshadri, Vijay. "Amy Clampitt's Dahlia Gardens."

Snively, Susan. "Amy Clampitt's Elegiac Witnessing."

Spiegelman, Willard. "What to Make of an Augmented Thing: Amy Clampitt's Syntactic Dramas."

Other Notable Essays

Goodridge, Celeste. "Reimagining 'Empire's Westward Course': Amy Clampitt's *A Silence Opens.*" In *Women Poets of the Americas: Toward a Pan-American Gathering.* Ed. Jacqueline Vaught Brogan and Cordelia Chávez Candelaria. Notre Dame, IN: University of Notre Dame Press, 1999.

Grogan, Ruth A. "Nobody Knows the Story: Amy Clampitt's Poems of Childhood." *Papers on Language and Literature,* Fall 2004.

Salter, Mary Jo. Foreword, *The Collected Poems of Amy Clampitt.* New York: Alfred A. Knopf, Inc., 1997.

Spiegelman, Willard. "A Poet's Life in Letters." In *Love, Amy: The Selected Letters of Amy Clampitt.* New York: Columbia University Press, 2005.

Vendler, Helen. "Amy Clampitt." In *The Music of What Happens: Poems, Poets, Critics.* Cambridge, MA: Harvard University Press, 1988.

Weisman, Karen A. "Starving Before the Actual: Amy Clampitt's 'Voyages: A Homage to John Keats.'" *Crit* 36.1 (1994).

Interview

Among many interviews Clampitt gave, the most complete and revealing is "The Art of Poetry XLV," conducted by Robert E. Hosmer, Jr., *Paris Review* 126 (Spring 1993).

Index of Titles

A NOTE ABOUT THE EDITOR

Mary Jo Salter is the author of six collections of poetry. She is Andrew W. Mellon
Professor in The Writing Seminars at Johns Hopkins University, and divides her time be-
tween Baltimore, Maryland, and Amherst, Massachusetts.

A NOTE ON THE TYPE

This book was set in Baskerville, a facsimile of the type cast from the original matrices
designed by John Baskerville. The original face was the forerunner of the modern group
of typefaces.

Composed by Creative Graphics,
Allentown, Pennsylvania

Printed and bound by Thomson-Shore, Inc.
Dexter, Michigan